WATERFOWL CARVING
with J.D. Sprankle

Waterfowl Carving

with J.D. SPRANKLE

The fully illustrated reference to
carving and painting 25 decorative ducks

ROGER SCHROEDER
and
JAMES D. SPRANKLE

STACKPOLE BOOKS

Published by
STACKPOLE BOOKS
5067 Ritter Road
Mechanicsburg, PA 17055

Cover photograph by Richard Meek.

First paperback printing, January 1995

10 9 8 7 6 5 4 3 2 1

First edition

Printed in the U.S.A.

Library of Congress Cataloging-in-Publication Data

Schroeder, Roger, 1945–
     Waterfowl carving with J.D. Sprankle.

     Bibliography: p.
          1. Sprankle, James D.   2. Waterfowl in art.
     3. Wood-carving—Technique.   4. Painting—Technique.
     I. Sprankle, James D.   II. Title.
     NK9798.S67S36   1985   731.4′62   85-9748
     ISBN 0-8117-3094-8

to Richard Meek, the teacher;
to Patricia Sprankle, the wife;
and to the people of Kent Island, Maryland.

Contents

Foreword

Competition has played such a prominent role in the history of American decorative bird carving that it is impossible when writing about it not to include Jim Sprankle. Jim is a competitor. His whole life has, in fact, involved competition and discipline. It is particularly his intense discipline that has allowed him to succeed in nearly anything he has wanted to accomplish.

In the early 1970s Jim became interested in bird carving. Studying under the legendary Ken Harris in Woodville, New York, Jim quickly found a place in the decoy tradition that would later lead to the decorative art form.

From the first decoy contest, held in 1876 by George Brown Good, the Deputy Secretary of the Smithsonian Institution, to today's World Championship Carving Competition sponsored by the Ward Foundation, the tool of the bird hunt, the decoy, has been evaluated in a sportsman's atmosphere. It was into this environment that Jim, a waterfowl hunter himself, easily moved in 1971. Since that time he has won a multitude of ribbons in bird carving competitions across the United States.

But after only a few years, Jim's birds could no longer be looked upon as the tools a hunter would use to bring a duck into the range of a gun. Jim was making his waterfowl to catch people, not ducks, and to float on a table or mantel, not on water.

Working fourteen-hour days, he is able, today, to produce a finely carved duck that is virtually impossible to tell from a live one. The techniques he has developed over the years have been major contributions toward the improvement of bird carving.

When looking at a Jim Sprankle carving, his style, his unique skill, and his way of visualizing the world around him become readily apparent. For Jim does more than just handle the sculpting tools that remove material to form another object. He creates an identity which comes from the head and not just the hand. With years of observation and a deep love of the waterfowl, he brings life to birds in wood.

Kenneth Basile
Museum Director, The Ward Foundation

Introduction

The largest tidal estuary on the North American continent is the Chesapeake. Very close to 200 miles in length and 30 miles at its widest, it is a mixture of salt and fresh water that the Indians called Chesepiooc, an Algonquin name meaning the Great Shellfish Bay. Apart from the shell- and finfish, and the 13 million people who live in the Bay's watershed, there are at least one million Canada geese that find a winter home there.

Located in the upper part of the Bay is Kent Island which with its parallel Bay bridges, connects the eastern and western shores of Maryland. U.S. 50 runs across the island with its two motels, a handful of restaurants, and no McDonald's. The nearest city to it is Annapolis. At the southern end of this island shaped like a withered hand is a bay called Eastern Bay. Rafts of Canadas rest there, their numbers on a winter's day reaching upwards of 5,000 or more. At night their chesty calls dominate the air, and it is unlikely that those living near the water do not hear those sounds which greet the morning sunrise.

That bay-within-a-bay is where I spent a number of weekends during the winter of 1984 and 1985, a guest of Jim Sprankle. This book, then, is the story not of the Chesapeake but of this man who built his home on Eastern Bay. He is a person who, nearly all his life, has sought the water's edge for housing, for hunting, for watching waterfowl. So the bays and rivers he hunted and lived on have shaped his thinking, and ultimately his choice of profession. Jim Sprankle is a carver by trade. No, he is not the carver of folkart figures with chipped-away faces and pen-knifed limbs. Instead, he is a maker of waterfowl, giving them every attention to detail he can possibly achieve. Feathers are not only delineated, but they are also given quill and barb lines, and finally colored with meticulously mixed paints to replicate the colors of the living birds. And delicate primary feathers jut out from his birds' backs, while relaxed eyes peer out from wood that has the look of downy head feathers.

Jim is also a competitor. He has taken his carved waterfowl to the Pacific Coast, to the Midwest, to New England, and he has returned home with enough blue ribbons to cover a sizable wall.

Jim Sprankle, whose careers have ranged from baseball to wildfowl carving, is noted for his intensity and competitiveness. Here he works on a gadwall drake in his painting room.

He is well known in the bird-carving world, especially to those who attend the prestigious World Championship Wildfowl Carving Competition sponsored by the Ward Foundation of Salisbury, Maryland. There he has taken over seventy First Place blue ribbons and numerous Best-in-Show awards for his birds.

But I did not meet Jim Sprankle at the World Championships, held each spring in Ocean City, Maryland's Convention Hall. We had our first meeting at his previous home in Annapolis in the fall of 1983. I was authoring a book about the techniques of nine of North America's top wildfowl carvers. Having studied his consistently winning record through such publications as the *Ward Foundation News*, I had no trouble choosing him to be one of the nine. We spent two weekends together, sharing and photographing his skills with carving and texturing tools, taking pictures of his carvings, recording his thoughts about the art form.

A special treat was a chance to enter Jim's own aviary, a wire enclosure in which he keeps live birds

for use as study aids. I think, though, they have been as much friends to him as teachers of avian behavior and appearance.

I kept in touch with Jim until my book *How to Carve Wildfowl* was published by Stackpole Books in September 1984. At that time, he was in the process of moving east of Annapolis to some island I had never heard of, somewhere in the middle of the Chesapeake. He said his new home would be smaller, but it would afford a daily and three-sided view of the water. He had mentioned during our talks that a book devoted solely to his carving might be well received by others interested in mastering waterfowl carving.

We worked quickly to write a proposal, and only two weeks after *How to Carve Wildfowl* had been released, we contracted to do this book. It was somehow fitting that signatures were inked in the Salisbury Civic Center where the Ward Foundation was holding its Wildfowl Carving and Art Exhibition. This was no hall of mirrors, but instead a place of finely displayed carvings and paintings.

Jim had on his table what has become one of his finest pieces—a black duck, its webbed foot extended to its head, one small nail of a toe brushing through the wooden feathers of the duck's basswood cheek. There was no doubt in my mind that Jim had a great deal to offer to a book.

We spent, then, weekends together to create *Waterfowl Carving with J.D. Sprankle*. This was to be a project book, a photographic essay of how birds take shape from bulky blocks of basswood, his favorite wood; how they take on anatomy and details; and finally (and literally) how they molt from a bland base of white priming paint to their acrylic colors. We spoke to our editor of doing five birds. But we decided after the first day of working together to devote most of the book to one. It's a male bird, and it is one of the most beautifully colored ducks I have seen—a gadwall drake.

What has resulted from our efforts are nearly two hundred and fifty photos of the drake coming alive from Jim's skilled hands with my still-framing every significant cut, burn line, and brush stroke with my camera. The photos are exhaustive, and hopefully, they lead you every step of the way from block to finished gadwall with neither guessing nor ambiguity as to what is happening. Hands-at-work photos are what I call them, and they are mixed with posed shots of the bird as details fill up the once-smooth wood.

I believe there to be so much information with this

What Jim describes as a "competition bird" is this black duck, carved in 1984 for the Ward Foundation's World Championship Wildfowl Carving Competition. It took First Place in Species.

The focal point of this book of technique is this gadwall drake, carved during the fall and winter of 1984. Nearly two hundred and fifty photos take the reader from beginning block to painted duck.

one project, in photos and text, that to essay even one more duck from beginning to end would be redundant. There are subtle differences, though often dramatic ones in terms of color, that can best be researched from photos of live birds, visits to aviaries, good taxidermy mounts, and other study aids.

Still, to appease those who might see this as a gadwall book, I photographed other birds in various stages of completion as well as finished pieces. These, with the gadwall, should help the carver build up a mastery of shaping, texturing, and burning techniques. Plus, there are patterns, eye sizes, and painting instructions for twenty-five birds from gadwall to black duck to baikal teal.

I would hope that the carver will find this a reference of tips on tools and techniques that will make carving almost any waterfowl possible. As Jim told me so often, a carving is only as good as the reference material used. And I should think a beginning carver of waterfowl will learn from the book just where to look for those subtle differences in ducks, from mandibles to tertials to specula to nubbins. It is a textbook, then, for the beginner, for the professional, for the artist.

Yet, I see this as more than another how-to text. It is also a story of a carver's life, his studies, his discipline, his devotion to and sometimes his obsession with his art. Sharing those weekends with him and his family

Another project described through photos is painting this cinnamon teal drake. This was carved for the 1985 World Championships during the same period the gadwall was carved. Like the gadwall, it is a floating decorative piece.

Yet another duck that can be glimpsed in various stages is this canvasback drake.

This head of a gadwall drake, carved in 1983, shows a delicate yet complex pattern of head streaks and cupped feathers, making this a challenging project for any carver. This, as well as the techniques needed to shape the head and bill and set the eyes, is covered in this book.

brought to focus more than black-and-white poses and hands-on images. I ate breakfast with him, always before eight in the morning. I watched him feed the ducks in his aviary, ones he had brought with him from Annapolis. I shared thoughts with him about other carvers I have met. I stood at his shoulder and breathed in the same wood dust he inhaled. I watched the same sunrises and sunsets he loved to observe. And I shared my love of wood and tools with Jim Sprankle.

Briefly, since this is not my story, I have been working with wood for the last fifteen years of my life. Basic bookcases evolved into corner cabinets which evolved into more elaborate pieces of furniture, some

carved, but all designed by me. As I write, I sit at a hand-carved Chippendale desk I created from rough-sawn planks of mahogany. I combined, then, carving and cabinetmaking to surround myself with my craft. But I also teach high school English, and, like many of my departmental colleagues, I yearn to write. It seemed natural, then, to bring together wood and words and become a technical writer in the wood-working field. I have contributed to national wood-working magazines, have been a contributing editor of one, and have interviewed fellow woodworkers and wood carvers.

One of the true bird-sculpting geniuses, whom I interviewed for a magazine article, is a young iconoclast named Grainger McKoy. When I met him in 1980 in his South Carolina studio, his largest sculpture was taking shape. It was a covey of quail, comprising no less than thirteen birds breaking into flight. My interest in birds was whetted. And that experience helped with the Stackpole connection. An editor and her publishing house had enough faith to ask me to write and photograph *How to Carve Wildfowl*. By the time I finished the book, I had found myself, in the words of one of the book's nine artists, Gary Yoder, "in the mainstream of bird carving."

This book too is a collaboration, perhaps a symmetry, of many efforts and talents. First, there had to be an amicable synchronization of actions, with Jim's carving, texturing, and painting and my taking photos and listening. Then there was Judith Schnell's intensive editing and honing of the manuscript and her laborious job of overseeing the smooth production of a manuscript that becomes a book.

And there was input from Richard Meek, one of today's most skilled professional photographers. His help is beyond value.

But I would add that few feelings override those of being accepted, I, a stranger on a strange island. The people I met on Kent Island, Jim's friends, neighbors, and acquaintances, accepted me with a graciousness that goes beyond Northern or Southern hospitality. Kent Islanders like Billy Comegys added another dimension to the relationship between carver and writer. To him and the others, Jim and I are grateful.

Before I can let you move on to the photos and text, I would point out that there is a controversy, or rather a minor skirmish, among critics of carved birds as to whether they encompass an art form. We do know their origins are uniquely American, with Indians setting out decoys made of bulrushes and feathers as far back as a millenium ago. But the industrious settlers and colonists chose wood for a medium, got more imitative, more colorful with their birds until the great names like the Veritys of Seaford, New York, Elmer Crowell of East Harwich, Massachusetts, the Ward Brothers (the Ward Foundation honors them) of Crisfield, Maryland, and others added their own subtleties to what were once roughly shaped birds made of materials as unusual as roots and cork. So bills became delicate, colors and vermiculation were finely painted, and shapes took on character with heads turned and wings defined. The crafting of birds had become decorative.

It was not until the 1970s, however, that carvers like McKoy got the once flat-bottomed decoy off its feet and into the air. Feathers were no longer slashes of paint but were now defined with burning and grinding tools. Many were even made of separate pieces of wood and inserted into bodies.

True, these are mechanics, but they are no different from those of the stone sculptor who, if seen at the early stages of his work, would appear as little more than a common laborer. But the results of his efforts may be, according to the critics, highly artistic.

My notion of an artist, then, is one who looks for shapes and colors and then brings them together uniquely, innovatively. This is what Jim does. He puts into his birds all those techniques that, if seen individually, would seem almost mechanical.

Jim has preferred to keep the bird out of the air and in the water where, hollowed, it could float. Jim was one of those carvers who kept the original form of the decoy, but brought to it his own artistic techniques and those of his carving peers.

In a field of highly decorative birds with wings outstretched and surrounded by metallic and synthetic habitat, his work may seem understated. Many of his pieces have flat bottoms, some have only stubs for legs, only a few have wings off the bodies. But Jim brings to his carvings a commitment to accuracy, while at the same time he looks for new forms to express his subject matter. His ducks are, so to speak, frozen in time as they drink from imaginary ponds, preen wood feathers, and occasionally scratch their faces. No quill is left unrendered, no bill wrinkle observable by his trained eye is left uncarved. What he brings to his carvings is a depth, perhaps an emotional presence, that begs you to pick up the bird, feel its textures, and look into its glass eyes.

I also believe that what Jim and others do is triumph over a medium, wood, that is inconsistent in its strength, lacks true solidity because of its cells, and has a capricious grain that makes working it at times seem impossible. But it is much more than mastering wood that sets Jim apart from carvers who craft figures. Jim has been inspired by living birds just as an artist is inspired by a model. Yet, it is a more intimate bond. He feeds his birds, photographs them, watches their every activity, looks for their personalities, even brings them into his shop. He is an aviculturist, and his aviary is as much a part of his art as is the medium of wood.

Another hallmark of his artistry, not unique to most creative people but essential to him, is discipline. His

Jim's meticulous attention to detail can be seen in the feathers of a carved black duck. Note the careful layout of barb and quill lines.

days are tightly scheduled and routined with meal breaks set by the clock. I see this organization as part of his success. His discipline has dovetailed well with his competitiveness to create so many fine birds, and the judges seem to agree. With nine years of profes-

Perhaps one million geese winter on the Chesapeake. Thousands can be seen flying over Jim's house on a single day.

sional carving behind him, Jim has received some two hundred and fifty blue ribbons.

As much as I enjoyed photographing Jim at work and his finished birds, I have to admit that the camera is inadequate. To appreciate his art, the finesse of his carvings, you should have the opportunity to hold them in your hands as I did. There were mergansers, harlequins, black ducks, gadwalls, teal. I felt the textures, ran my hands along the inserted feathers, saw the glints of reflected light in their lifelike eyes. I have no doubt now, if I ever did, that what Jim and others of his caliber do is art. Hopefully you will agree.

You begin with a biography that takes you from Lafayette, Indiana, to upstate New York, and finally to the Chesapeake. There you can watch and listen to migrating geese, feel the warmth of a winter sun reflected on the great estuary. Inside Jim's shop, you can watch wood disappear from a solid block of basswood that Jim brought from a lumber mill near Binghamton, New York. Later, the noise of the grinding tools is replaced by the heat of burning pens as the sharpness of knives puts in finer details. And finally you can watch the watery acrylics of the last stages of his art build up minutely to create the colors that help make wildfowl special to us.

Perhaps that helps answer a question so often asked: why the almost endemic interest in wildfowl? I think appearance is one answer. Even the black duck, with its monotonous dark brown color is attractive. Are birds friendly? Hitchcock's hostile birds are cinema fiction. Of course they are amicable. Have not most of us fed them at community ponds? That makes waterfowl, in particular, recognizable, another criterion for this animal's popularity.

Before I take you into Jim's shop, I should dispel

Jim's home is on Eastern Bay, a diminutive part of the larger Chesapeake. Owing in part to sunsets such as this, he is in love with his surroundings. The photo was taken from just outside his shop entrance.

any notions that this disciplined artist is an angry one, shut away in his studio, annoyed by any and all visitors. To the contrary, his door is unlocked to a host of people on any one day, all of whom generate a kind of warmth. I have met his friends, neighbors, hunters peeking in to see what bird Jim was working on, while quietly asking questions or sharing stories of what was taken from the skies . . . or what wasn't.

I recall in particular a dentist-hunter who came in to visit Jim one afternoon, a large man with immense hands that protruded from the sleeves of a camouflage jacket. He had won a canvasback Jim had carved for Ducks Unlimited, an organization that raises money to save Canadian wetlands, where nearly seventy percent of all wild ducks of the four American flyways are hatched. The carving was purchased by Ducks Unlimited and raffled off to raise funds.

The dentist-hunter, who talked first of his profession, and then of his gunning along the Chesapeake, finally asked Jim what the bird's worth was. Jim's figure held no surprise for me. I was well aware of the value of decorative carvings. The dentist-hunter wasn't. His almost giant frame jerked perceptibly.

I think this story offers a moral. It speaks of the worth of a man's work that takes up half the hours in a day, with as many as fourteen to twenty days needed to complete a carved waterfowl. And it suggests some shifting of values as to what these carvings are worth artistically and monetarily, and prompts a closer examination of the artistic statements made in wood.

Now you are ready to join me on Kent Island where each morning I passed there I was treated to an orange, red-rimmed earth at sunrise, and there was only one sunset during the same days that failed to exhibit an equally awesome display of reds brushed fully across a western horizon.

I remember looking out into the Eastern Bay and seeing what looked like exposed salt marshes in the distance, then seeing the land turn into waterfowl, taking flight in a flurry of noisy pinions.

I will never quite forget that eerie staccato call of a cinnamon teal hen outside the workshop, nor the wood duck that flew squarish circles around the perimeter of the aviary.

Share Jim's and my romance of Kent Island, then come indoors and watch a gadwall come to life.

1

The Story
of a Professional Carver

On Eastern Bay

Route 301 passes through some 100 miles of Maryland before it becomes Highway 50, the route to and across the Bay Bridge going toward Annapolis. As signs mark down the miles to the twin spans, one hardly notices the Kent Narrows Bridge, more an overpass than a span of steel and girders. For Kent Island is really a peninsula eroded away from the mainland by a channel of water. The transition between the two land masses is so smooth and level that you would not know you were on an island.

One of the three traffic lights that legally divide up Kent Island's portion of Highway 50 indicates Cox's Neck Road, a four-mile stretch of rolling, buckling blacktop through once-farmland properties. Near its end, flat, painted-in-grays-and-blacks wooden geese are posted notices of the Sprankles and their neighbors. A right turn onto a compacted oyster shell road and a half-mile of driving brings you to another sign. It is a readily recognizable, half-in-the-round canvasback duck, part of a larger sign that indicates the Sprankle home.

Beyond that, across a still-tilled pastureland is a gray, vertically sided house. It is clearly the newest home in the area, built in 1984. Two hundred feet to its left, across a driveway made white by crushed oyster shells, is a smaller gray building, Jim Sprankle's workshop. Butting one wall is a pen for his Labrador retriever, Teal. On the opposite side is a larger pen which shelters his ducks. If you had visited there in the fall and winter of 1984, you would have seen an extension to the shop take shape, a place for teaching. But more on that later.

The view, the property, the house are all magnificent, all of great worth to Jim, who, with his wife Patricia, designed the cedar house.

They will tell you that it was planned to capture, visually, as much of Eastern Bay as possible. From the living room, from the kitchen, from what they call the duck room, there is a panorama of water and waterfowl to be seen. Geese, marsh and diving ducks, and even a bald eagle might be seen on any given fall or winter day. And this is complemented not only by what is in Jim's aviary but also what is within the house. Nearly fifty waterfowl paintings, most in the

This is where Jim does his waterfowl carving. Along with the house, this shop was built in 1984 on Eastern Bay and measures 24 x 30 feet. The plastic-enclosed area to the right is his aviary in which Jim keeps live ducks for study.

duck room, rise up into a cathedral ceiling, giving color to the house's white walls and partially pine-beamed ceiling.

But this room is more than a gallery for the prints and watercolors he collects, many original and re-marqued by their artists. This area also provides display space for nearly one hundred carvings, more than half being his own. It is a growing collection on darkly stained pine shelves that he adds to each year, adding to it one waterfowl he has carved. And there are vintage pieces, antiques almost, and even the first decoy Jim carved, the first winner of a blue ribbon, the first floating decorative duck.

But being a woodworker, I found his separate workshop more appealing. There was, then, no musty basement in which to make sawdust, no grimy garage to paint in. Instead, a building was designed solely for the execution of wildfowl carvings.

If you had visited Jim in his Annapolis home, you would have found his workshop confined to the garage. On Kent Island, you would experience that peculiar feeling of having encountered the same situation previously. *Deja vu*, it is called. You were back in Annapolis, you would think. It is the same shop! you would exclaim. But the aviary outside the windows is no illusion, nor is the bay, and Jim would tell you that the shop's arrangement is the same. The dimensions of the carving room and the painting room are almost identical to those of the Annapolis rooms; they vary less than a foot.

As with the Annapolis arrangement, there is a room which houses heavy power equipment, a tablesaw and jointer, and a tall supply of basswood planks.

Jim's property, like that of many people on Kent Island, had once been a farm; it is now divided into lots and housed. According to a friend of Jim's, Toady Freeman, a bayman who has lived on the Chesapeake for more than sixty years, "Thirty-five years ago this island was all tomatoes, cucumbers, cantaloupes, and watermelons. But these vegetables gave way to corn and soybeans, and these foods attracted the geese." Toady also says, "I used to quail hunt here on the island, taking a ferry from Annapolis. We also shot scaup, black ducks, and mallards. They were here by the thousands, clouds of them in the fields." But, as he went on to tell me, the environment had changed, making it hospitable for geese, not ducks, looking for corn stubble and waste.

And both Toady and Jim will tell you that Kent Island was never a hotbed of decoy carving, though the Chesapeake itself was a breeder of carvers. Toady recalls that, in addition to Jim, there was once a farmer carving his own birds.

Decoys were made at the opposite ends of the Chesapeake. At the upper end are the Susquehanna Flats, and at the lower is Crisfield, home of the Ward Brothers who bequeathed so much to the decorative decoy makers. But probably more decoys came from the Flats, which lay between the Bay and the mouth of the Susquehanna River, and which was one of the most active gunning areas in this country. Gunning rigs numbered as many as five hundred decoys.

Despite the changes in farming and the dissolution of market hunting activities, which required so many wooden birds, Jim will point out canvasbacks he sees fly by, an occasional ring-necked duck, a goldeneye. These are the birds he knows, ones he has carved with unerring detail.

As I made my trips from one island, my home being on Long Island, to another, loaded with camera equipment, tape recorder, and film, I began to see this book as a tribute, and one that would perhaps bridge the gulf between pure technique and biography, as most technical books do not. The book would be well photographed, that went without statement. But I hoped that a portrait of a wildfowl artist would also emerge.

By the time the project was nearing completion, I saw Jim Sprankle as a man of humor and sincerity, with a personality that attracted people like children to the piper. Yet he could vary even within an hour, from being reserved to being a shouter and back to a muted observer. Also, I heard a cadence in his voice that suggested integrity and respect for what others do and say. But I was most aware of his intensity and alertness, which were visible even from a distance, even through the camouflage jacket he wrapped himself in to feed his ducks or to walk along the trim of sand left on the shore by diminutive tides. Here was a man who didn't waste actions, a trait he carried directly into the shop by eight each morning.

Ball Playing, Taxidermy, Banking, Refrigeration, Carving

But what of Jim's origins? What is the background of a man who carves professionally, creating no fewer than thirty full-size pieces each year? And what influences were there to bring him so much recognition and success, so many blue ribbons, and so many followers in the form of friends and students?

He was christened James Donald Sprankle, the only son of Max and Lou Ellen Sprankle. Misleadingly, he would tell you that life began for him on his eighteenth birthday when he signed to play professional baseball with the then Brooklyn Dodgers. It was during that same year that he graduated from Lafayette, Indiana's Jefferson High School. And at the end of each baseball season, he would return to Lafayette to attend classes in forestry and physical education at Purdue University and to work in a sporting goods store. He even found work in winter as a hunting guide in Canada. But selling baseball gloves was not to last long, nor did he believe that playing baseball would last forever. How, then, did he turn to wildfowl carving?

Since life did not begin when he was eighteen, we have to look to the years prior to his playing ball. He told me that in his early teens, a close friend named John Walkey, a leading authority on waterfowl, got him "all fired up with waterfowl hunting back in Indiana. And if you can get enthused there, you're really enthused." He added, parenthetically, "I see more waterfowl here on Kent Island than I did two or three whole seasons in Indiana. I guess we went out because we really loved it."

What might be called the first step toward professional carving was taken. But another one was fast in the making. At the age of sixteen, he became a licensed taxidermist, so part of the reason to go hunting was to get specimens to mount. "That and hunting," Jim explained, "gave me a view of what a bird should look like anatomically." He could not tell me for sure how many birds he mounted, but he was certain that there was one for every species of waterfowl he hunted.

Trying to show how past events and patterns of behavior brought him to where he is today, he said: "I've been interested in ducks since I was a young boy, and I've always loved the water, where you find ducks. I think they're colorful, I think they're interesting. At one time they were flying targets, though today I'd prefer to watch them than shoot them. But that exposure to taxidermy added a dimension to what I do now."

But there was yet another interest and talent that transected these previous two. In Jim's words, he was "exposed at an early age to woodworking. My grandfather was a cabinetmaker from Germany, and I more or less grew up in his shop. And though I was doing nothing I'm doing now, I was exposed to power tools and woods." At one time in his life, he built kitchen cabinets for customers on weekends and evenings. Other work included making gun cabinets for a sporting goods department store. And he even framed a house or two.

A hunter, Jim need go only five hundred feet from his house either to watch or shoot ducks and geese in this duck blind of reeds.

And what became of Purdue? "I found it harder and harder to return to college after each baseball season," he said. "I reached a point where I'd rather be working out in the fieldhouse than in the classroom. Also, new friends were made on the road, which helped break ties with Indiana." By the time he had finished with baseball, he was ready to move permanently. But, "Lafayette has some fond memories because it's where I started baseball. It was a sports-minded town, and Purdue University was a motivating place for sports-minded kids."

What he described as "another cycle" of his life was a move to Binghamton, New York, and to a new career. It was there that he started work for the Marine Midland Bank. As he pointed out, "Baseball doesn't prepare you for a whole lot. I was wise enough to know that when I was twenty-nine years old. The more I played ball, the harder it would be to start a new career. Baseball doesn't prepare you for much unless you coach or scout."

He recalled of banking: "I thought of a bank as just a place where you could cash a check or have a savings account. I didn't know you could buy a car or house through a bank." But he took banking courses and enjoyed doing public relations work for Marine Midland. When it came time to embark on yet another career, he left the bank as vice-president after six years.

It was through a banking connection that he met Dwight Harris of Apalachin, New York. It was Harris who brought Jim into the commercial refrigeration business, giving him the financial backing required. "I'll thank him until the day I die for that," Jim said, "for it was another challenge I truly enjoyed."

This goldeneye was the first hunting decoy Jim ever carved. Done in 1971, it was used for gunning on the St. Lawrence River, where he had a summer home.

Remnants of these careers are present today in his home and shop. In the kitchen against one wall is a bench made of American Ash – with baseball bats, canvas bases for bench seats, baseballs for finials. In the shop is a Sanolite cutting block used by butchers, and refrigeration fluorescents above his painting bench.

It was what Jim describes as a serious operation that changed his attitudes and career goals more than any other acquaintance or event. It was in 1976 that he underwent surgery with many months of recovery. A decision was soon set. "If I lived to be a hundred years old, or live only another two, I was going to do something the rest of my life I would really enjoy." He added quickly, however, that "It's not that I didn't enjoy baseball or banking or the refrigeration business. I did, and I know how fortunate I was never to have experienced a job where I hated to get up in the morning." It was, then, in 1976 that Jim started carving full-time.

It should be noted that waterfowl hunting was not left behind in Lafayette when he moved to upstate New York, where he lived in Conklin, a suburb of Binghamton, on the Susquehanna River for fifteen years. Weekends were spent traveling north to one of the Thousand Islands of the St. Lawrence River. He said those days were an important part of his life. "As soon as the ice would go out in the spring, I would hunt right up to December 15 until we were almost iced out at that point."

Did hunting, taxidermy, woodworking, business acumen, and an operation combine spontaneously to produce a highly regarded waterfowl carver? It was not in 1976 that Jim picked up carving tools for the first time. That had been done six years earlier.

At that time, he was not satisfied with store-bought gunning stool or decoys. Instead, he carved for his hunting rigs decoys with heads turned to one side or the other, getting the "stiffness" out of poses, putting a bit more realism into the birds.

Interestingly, it was not a hunting trip to the St. Lawrence but south to Tangier Island, Maryland, that must be credited with moving Jim in the direction of competitions and eventually some two hundred and fifty blue ribbons.

He had met some hunters there from (without any of the irony it deserves) Kent Island. These men suggested that he bring his decoys to the World Championships. Jim related that he'd had no idea that such a competition existed. In fact, his first entries were brought to the U.S. National Decoy Show, held on Long Island, New York. He had put his birds in the amateur division, only to be disappointed. "I didn't know that ducks would be floated, and all mine were solid. I guess I got two or three honorable mentions, but I did learn that you have to hollow my kind of birds for those shows."

He also recalled that decoys could have neither fragile tails nor primaries that extended from the body. They had to be the traditional self-righting gunning decoys or they would face disqualification. It was within a year or two of his first show that judging was relaxed, and decorative aspects were encouraged.

A Sense of Place

As might be deduced, Jim did not move to Kent Island directly from New York. The first move was to Annapolis in 1980. Four years after that, with a new house constructed, he made what he calls his final move, to Maryland's Eastern Shore.

I was curious to know, as we sat in his shop one morning, he burning in detail on the gadwall, I listening to the hunters in a nearby duck blind bring geese down in the remarkably still water of Eastern Bay, how the Chesapeake compared to his homes in Indiana and New York. He told me that his present home has re-created many of the feelings he had at the other

In 1973, Jim carved this bluebill drake. Now in his private collection, it was his first decorative carving.

Jim won his first blue ribbon with this black duck. Also in his collection, it was carved in 1974.

two. "You see seasons change and migrating water-fowl. These, to me, constitute a lasting memory of an area. But Kent Island is completely different from those other two places. Here you wake up in the morning and see thousands of waterfowl outside your window, even a hundred feet from the house. It's a great feeling and hard to beat. And though motivation is not something I need, seeing all this doesn't hurt." He added, "It's exciting to see, even if you're not a waterfowler."

There was no denying any of this. On my first morning on Kent Island in November of 1984, I was awakened to a thunderous sound of geese greeting the dawn. Looking out my bedroom window to see them, I recall a certain suspension of time, for I could see no other houses, no boats, no hunters in sight. I wondered if this was what settlers so many generations before mine had seen.

A Man of Many Headlines

Jim had given me homework to do between visits. It was to read articles from newspapers and magazines about him. From New York, from Maryland, from the Ward Foundation, the headlines were clever, suggestive of his varied backgrounds. Some were: A Craftsman in Pursuit of Excellence; Dodger, Top Decoy Carver; Hunter Prefers Creating to Killing Ducks; Ducks, Decoys: Which is Which? Former Baseball Player Keeps Competitive Edge as Carver; Jim Sprankle . . . A Pro Turned Amateur. All the articles referred to his competitiveness, his many ribbons, the forty hours it would take him to complete a bird, his enjoyment of carving. One Maryland newspaper

noted that Jim would stay at his Conklin, New York, home for six weeks at a time, never leaving except to get a haircut.

Early articles referred to his hunting and taxidermy backgrounds. But over the years, a tempering of the hunter mentality occurred; the desire to mount one's trophies transpired. And while the number of ducks mounted each year increased, the photos indicated a growing realism from less-detailed birds to more anatomically perfect waterfowl.

One statement in particular I found interesting. It was in 1977 that he said, "I've never carved a bird I was satisfied with, and the day I do, it's time to get out of the competitive part of it." In that same year, he was quoted as saying: "I'd like to think I would be regarded as one of the better carvers. This is my life. Something of a constant challenge . . . and a pursuit of excellence."

Self-Discipline

Jim had a few pieces of his earliest work for me to see, stylized ducks, unburned and untextured, colors bright. But they were not as lifelike as those he achieves today, not stiff but lacking the subtle personality achieved with just a slightly raised head. I wondered, then, how he knew nine years earlier that he could turn bird carving into a full-time living?

He explained that in 1976 he had numerous orders for carved birds. "I knew I could earn enough without worrying about where my next meal was coming from. That's probably when I knew I was doing this professionally. But it's a gamble for some people," he admitted. "Yet I knew that self-discipline was the key."

Jim's evolution as a carver led to this piece, a black duck carved in 1981. A floating decorative piece, it took First Place in Species in the Midwest Decoy Contest. It is owned by Terry Smith of Rockville, Maryland.

Jim's attention to detail might seem dramatic in this carving of a pintail drake he did. Executed in 1984, it is owned by David Evans of Bethesda, Maryland.

Jim once pitched for the Brooklyn Dodgers. Now he uses his hands to shape wood. Here he works on a duck head with the popular grinding tool called the Foredom.

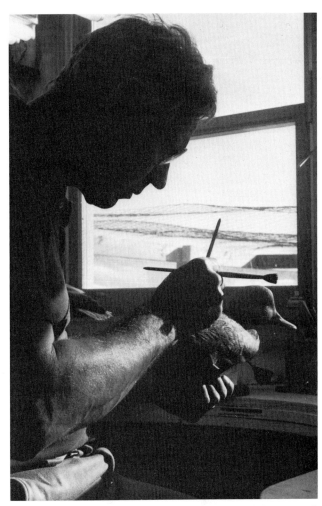

Jim's life has been described as a study of discipline and dedication, with his spending up to 14 hours a day carving and painting a bird. Here in his painting room he can look out into the aviary.

I've come to realize that this hyphenated word is one Jim uses more than any other to describe his personality. What does he mean by it? The answer is on two levels, one perhaps philosophical, the other dealing with daily realities. For the latter, he told me, "It means getting out to my shop every day at 8 a.m. stopping at noon for lunch, coming back out at 1 p.m. and working until 5:30. Then I can go back after dinner and work until 10:00."

The philosophical issues are obviously deeper. He talked about being dedicated to what he is doing, eliminating distractions from his life, such as not taking time off to play golf. When he takes a little time off to read, it might be a book or an article about naturalists and painters such as John Audubon and Louis Agassiz Fuertes. "I found that these were very dedicated men," he reflected. "I guess I've always advocated that to learn to be a wildlife artist, you have to dedicate a lot of your life to it. I believe that many people don't understand what it takes when they begin a career such as carving. But perhaps it takes a special person who can sit by himself day after day,

for hours on end, without stopping. Something like what I'm doing takes a tremendous amount of self-discipline and concentration and almost living your subject matter day and night."

He will even tell people who want to carve full-time: "You're going to have to sacrifice whatever you're doing now. You just can't pick this up and drop it, pick it up and drop the carving. When I started, it was no longer quite so important to go out and hunt every weekend. My priorities changed. Now I get just as much enjoyment being in a cold shop carving wildfowl as being in a duck blind."

Still, he does not lose sight of his end product, saying, "I try to make every carving something I'm proud of. I guess I'm carving to have something to live on after I die. It seems that a lot of people don't leave much behind after they've moved on. It's an expression of yourself . . . I guess I like to keep trying to do

Though he is not inhibited as a waterfowl hunter, he is more inclined to shoot ducks with his camera. Slides taken will later be turned into patterns for carvings. Here he sits in a concrete casting in his aviary, which allows him to photograph ducks at eye level.

good carving. I don't think anyone's opposed to being remembered after he's long gone."

Jim told me about a fellow bird carver named Ken Harris from Woodville, New York. Harris had two sons, both in business. Neither, he felt, would be remembered as long as the father who daily produced many fine gunning and decorative decoys.

The First Ducks

Jim has spent more than nine years now working almost daily, except during competitions and very short vacations or hunting trips away from home. During that time, he has carved more than seven hundred birds. I asked him about the first ones he sold. He instantly recalled that they were bought by his business partner in the refrigeration business, Dwight Harris. Jim explained the circumstances. "I had about five or six birds I'd carved, and Dwight wanted to buy them. What gave me trouble was trying to determine how much they were worth since I had never sold a bird before. And I had no idea what other birds were being marketed at. I asked $150 a bird, but Dwight came over a couple of days later with an envelope. In it was $1,500. It was nearly double what I had asked for. That really set the tone for the value of my birds back then. And very quickly after that, I sold birds to a friend in Binghamton. Both these men, I should note, were close friends, and I suspect that's the case with most carvers—the first couple of birds are sold or given to close friends or hunting buddies." I do not believe that Jim has had trouble selling a carved bird since.

Competition

Much of the literature about Jim points to his unmatched number of blue ribbons won, his Best-in-Show awards, his unmatched number of first-place ribbons taken at the World Championships. And he is not reticent about pointing out these wins. I asked him directly to talk about his competitiveness. His response was equally sharp and tautological.

"Anyone who enters competitions is competitive. You don't win if you're not. It's almost a requirement you have to have. If that weren't the case, you couldn't strive to do better. And if you strive to do better, you're competitive."

But Jim would seem to have some misgivings about competitions. "When I was with baseball, I wasn't taught to lose, and I knew what I had to do to win. Three strikes made an out, 27 outs made a game. In carving, it's more of a shootout. What I mean by that is, a competition doesn't always indicate how well a bird is carved. It's three judges' perceptions, and sometimes a carver knows as much or more about his bird than the judges do. So you have to accept defeat and hope you win your fair share."

Jim has won that share fairly, and blue ribbons have had no small impact on his business. "I don't think there's any question that blue ribbons help sell birds. In fact, there's a certain number of people I sell to who want just competition birds, no matter what species they are. That's got to tell you that part of my market is out to buy a winner."

Competition Birds and Upside-Down Geese

What exactly is a competition bird? Jim said during one weekend with me that he would be carving a competition bird beginning early in January and continuing through February. His wife had told me sympathetically that it would be a tense time for him, a time during which he could not face other pressures or distractions.

As a prelude to explaining why these birds might be different from others that he carves during the year, Jim said, "Most people will want to compete and will want to win. I think that makes for a better person. And though I'm not a philosopher, I believe Americans have always been involved in competitive things. So if you do birds that may be a little different,

This cinnamon teal drake is one of many competition birds Jim has carved for the World Championships. This took First Place in Species in 1984 and is owned by Nancy Belksy of Omaha, Nebraska. The pattern and pose of this bird were taken from an aviary slide.

with a different pose or attitude involved to catch the judges' eyes, that's a competition bird."

For the 1983 World Championship Wildfowl Carving Competition, Jim had done a ring-necked duck, a floating bird with one webbed foot out of the water. Another, a black duck in 1984, scratched a wooden foot against a cheek, the eye reactively squinting.

Jim stated, however, that he would never do an inferior bird, because customers would soon bring it to his attention when comparisons with other birds were made. He admitted, though, that "subconsciously, you try a little harder with your competition birds."

But Jim said again, almost as an aside, that sometimes judges do not understand what a carver is trying to achieve. "You know, I hate to hear from judges that a duck can't do this or that. They might better say that seldom would a duck do that. You should never say never because, invariably, if you're judging, someone will bring you a photograph to disprove you."

"I remember seeing a scolding widgeon pair carved by a friend of mine. When I got my first live widgeon pair, I remembered seeing that, and I had questioned him about the piece."

"I also remember seeing someone's painting of geese flying upside down, and you say that can't happen. But it does happen. I've seen it. In a courtship flight in the spring, geese will flip over 180 degrees. So don't say never. Things happen."

Hens for the Women

Since Jim is no neophyte to marketing practices, he is particularly skillful when it comes to selling his own carvings. He offered some interesting advice on selling.

"A big percentage of people will come to a show and not know one carving from another. It's important, then, for those people to remember you. Spend time with people, talk to them. And just because they may not be asking carving-related questions, don't think they're not prospective buyers."

What kinds of questions has Jim heard? The basic ones are: "'How much does that bird cost? What's it carved out of? How many birds can you carve in a year?' Those questions are invariable and almost in that order," Jim told me. "A part of carving is being able to meet people and to merchandise yourself and your carvings. So, since many of those people are exposed to carving for the first time, be friendly, answer questions, and you'll have a better chance of being remembered after they leave the show."

I asked if people prefer some species of ducks over others. He said, "I sell and get orders for whatever is at my table, so it behooves me to try to do as many different species a year as possible. But invariably, a woman will want a hen. I guess it goes with more decors than some of the gaudy birds like wood ducks. But I'll even do one or two of those a year. It's impor-

Jim finds that women prefer buying hens. He has learned that the coloration of the hens, usually shades of brown, go with more decors. This hooded merganser hen was carved in 1984.

tant to do an occasional bird like this if for nothing more than to refresh my mind on what the bird looks like. It even helps when judging."

The Ward Foundation and Hands-On Seminars

What Jim told me had held true at the Salisbury Exhibition, where we signed contracts to do this book. There I watched a neatly but unpretentiously dressed man, smiling behind a table of some of his most recent and best carvings, the showpiece being, perhaps, that deftly scratching black duck. He appeared to know more people than any other carver. We had little time to talk because there were so many people stopping by to greet him—personal friends, acquaintances, people who had seen his work at other shows.

Interestingly, the Salisbury show is not only a place for Jim to exhibit his work, but it is also the child of the Ward Foundation, which has become a marketplace of carving ideas and trends, and has aided the progression of bird carving from craft origins to art decorative.

Jim's remarks about the Foundation, which was founded in 1968, were laudatory. He called its World Championship Competition, not unexpectedly, "the World Series of carving." The Foundation also has a museum at Salisbury State College, containing its World Class Decorative Lifesize winners, one having been purchased each year of the contest. I would carry Jim's analogy a little further and call this museum the wildfowl carver's Hall of Fame.

"The Ward Foundation," Jim said, "has helped me in many ways. The simplest is that it has two functions I participate in, both the backbone of what I do. There's the sponsored spring show [held in Ocean City, Maryland], with its World Class categories. I think part of the reason our art form, if you're brave enough to call it that, has progressed so rapidly is because of that competition."

Jim went on to say that the fall show, held in Salisbury, provides a showplace for carvers to display their birds and for painters to exhibit wildfowl art. "There's no charge for the exhibitor, and it's another important marketplace for artists."

He added that the magazine published by the Ward Foundation, the *Ward Foundation News*, contains timely articles about carving techniques, features about carvers such as Jim, collecting, advertisements, and listings of events. "It offers ways for carvers to learn," Jim pointed out.

He went on to say that, "If someone asks me what carvings to collect, or how do I know what is good with a carving, I tell that person to call the Ward Foundation. To me, they're the last word, or the best place, for the new person interested in carvings to collect. And you'll get an updated, unbiased assessment." He added unabashedly that his name has been given as one whose carvings would provide a good investment. "Buying good carvings is like buying stock. Some will increase in value. I think mine will."

But according to Jim, one of the Ward Foundation's most valuable functions has been its seminars. Given before the World Class Competitions start, one-day seminars are offered each year by three carvers who share the best of their techniques with large audiences. In 1979, Jim gave what he described as a flip-chart presentation of how to create birds, from wood to burning and texturing, and finished with painting tips.

But the Ward Foundation has recently been sponsoring seminars in June that offer hands-on instruction to smaller classes of students. Jim first taught one in 1984. "Few things were as rewarding as that," he said. "I never saw such a group of attentive people wanting to learn carving. I saw 20 people whose intensity was unbelievable. We started at 8 a.m. and, with meal breaks, we worked into the next morning. I don't think I ever worked harder during a comparable span of time. I was drained after the five-and-a-half-day seminar was over. When I got home, I told my wife that we're going to add to this shop [the shop and the house were being constructed that summer]. I told her we should be teaching these seminars at home."

Jim will be teaching seminars by the time this book is printed. The shop addition was completed by the time Jim and I finished with each other. Jim's intent is to offer carving sessions, also five-and-one-half days in length, that will include pattern development and layout, shaping, burning, texturing, and eye placement. Another set of sessions will focus on painting, including color blending, airbrush use, and sequential painting. An explanatory letter written by Jim is included in the Appendix.

The responses I have seen indicate that the Sprankle seminars will be well received. At last count, carvers from such states as California, Idaho, Texas, Michigan, Florida, Illinois, Pennsylvania, Tennessee, Delaware, and Maryland had expressed a desire to journey to Jim's shop to learn.

Credits Due

Few carvers work without some input from others. Perhaps all waterfowl carvers owe some credit to Steve and Lemuel Ward for setting precedents with colors and poses that put their birds in such demand. Jim is no exception and is willing to credit those who helped him in his early stages of bird carving.

One of the first to aid him was Ken Harris (no relation to Dwight Harris). This man was many things, an insurance salesman, a musician, and a professional carver who produced thousands of birds, many of which command hundreds of dollars at antique decoy shows. He taught Jim much about shaping wood.

George Walker, who today lives in Chesterfield, New Jersey, was another mentor. It was he who sold Jim his first grinding tool, the Foredom, at a decoy show in Clayton, New York. Jim described Walker as one of the most generous people he has met in the carving business. And when Walker offered to show Jim how to use the tool, Jim did not hesitate to drive to New Jersey from upstate New York. "George was always quick to point out new things in carving," Jim recalled, "and he has helped so many people in this business."

Also crucial to his development as a wildfowl carver were Michigan artists Jim Foote and Larry Hayden. Both had aviaries: Hayden still has his, and he was the first North American bird carver to keep live birds. Both influenced Jim in establishing his own aviaries, the first being in Kirkwood, New York, in 1978.

Another carver Jim gives credit to, especially for constructive criticism, is John Scheeler of May's Landing, New Jersey. Winner of 30 Best-in-Show awards, Scheeler is a master of decorative wildfowl. A 1983 piece that won him the Best in World Decorative Life-size prize is a goshawk and crow, victor and victim in an astonishing display of realism. Jim said of Scheeler, almost reverentially, "No one captures life and death the way John Scheeler does."

But Jim credits men like Scheeler, Hayden, and Foote not only for their skills at carving and painting but also for what he calls "a retention for detail." He said, "Show something to one of these carvers, either on a live duck or on one of wood and paint, and he will remember most of what he sees." It is this retention that Jim feels is a characteristic of successful wildfowl carvers.

"I remember the many hours of help I've received from the Ken Harrises, the Larry Haydens, the George Walkers, and the John Scheelers. And since I haven't forgotten all their help, it's hard for me not to help others." Yet he admitted, "When you make a living at it, time is money. But I try to do my best when questions are asked. And many of those questions come from former seminar participants."

Jim said of carvers in general that there is a tendency for them to help one another, calling it "a sort of open fraternity." He added that the better carvers would seem to live in clusters or satellite areas, such as in Michigan where Foote and Hayden live, in southern Louisiana where people like master wildfowl carver Tan Brunet reside, and in pocket areas like Chincoteague or the Chesapeake. "You're particularly fortunate if you live in an area where better carvers live so you can get them to critique your work. It makes the learning process a lot simpler."

He also noted that there is a kind of leapfrogging effect among carvers. "Another carver can't give you much input until he knows what you know already. Then when he catches up, you'll be trying to keep a step ahead." This encourages the competitiveness that Jim speaks about so often.

Wildfowl Carver or Artist?

During one of our interviews, I wondered if I had been too liberal with my use of the term *artist*, and I asked Jim if he agreed with my assessment of him and others as artists. Jim's comments were somewhat unexpected. First, he said that he did not know the meaning of the term. "I think ninety percent of the

There may be a fine line between what is art and what is craft, but Jim's concerns are an unusual pose and a masterful attention to detail.

Jim says that this home will be his last, and that he will continue to carve as long as he is able to. Here he devotes time to the gadwall drake that is central to this book.

people who claim they're artists may not be. Second, I ask you, is an artist someone who works in an art-related medium? Who really knows? I just refer to myself as a wildfowl carver." He added, however, that art is no more than what people perceive it to be. "The owner of a piece of work has to determine whether what I'm doing is art or craft."

He seemed to have some qualifying thoughts, for he went on to say, "I like to think of what I am doing as an art form. I'm not a craftsman out here in my studio making pottery. Yet, most people in the art world look at us as second-class citizens. But I'll tell you this. At some wildfowl festivals, more people are lined up to see the carvers than the painters of waterfowl.

"But who really has the final, the ultimate, word? I think historians out of museums will make that judgment. The Ward Foundation calls this an art form. And I'm not going to disagree with them."

"What More Would I Want?"

When the gadwall was nearly completed and paints were nearly dried on it, Jim decided to give me what amounted to a summary of his life. He began by saying, "When I was growing up, the only thing I ever thought about was playing professional baseball. And only one boy out of millions ends up doing that or playing another professional sport. And even though I told you that sports don't prepare you for much, I don't doubt that it prepared me for the competitiveness of what I do. And when I was in business, I tried to hire people who had some kind of sports background, people who had a taste for winning."

I remember that Jim looked up at me at that moment, serious in his choice of words and said, typical of his philosophy that joins competitive gamesmanship with long-term success, "You've been writing books. And no doubt you want to do better than the next guy writing. So in theory there's a game going on that you want to win, that is, by selling twice as many books as your competitor. And this is what I want. So sports prepared the way for my public relations job with a bank, and that prepared me for the business of selling birds. And that will be my last job."

He paused again. "You asked me once if what I do is an obsession. It is with me. It's part of my makeup. But it's got to be in other carvers like John Scheeler. I think that's why he's been the very best for so many years."

He went on to talk about the present, saying, "I feel fortunate that I can get up every morning and come out to the shop and work. I watched my father struggle through life, getting up every morning without ever being very excited, working at an aluminum plant. And I'm also fortunate to be working on this bay, a little piece of heaven, perhaps. Tan Brunet, who visited me recently, said, 'You can hunt here, you can sleep here, you can work here. What more would you want?' That's very true. What more would I want?"

2

References:
From Aviary to Molded Birds

"I don't think carved birds are going to get more realistic looking, because you can only bring them so far," Jim said. Yes, I know what I'm doing is not really like the good Lord made them, but I do believe that we're reaching a point where we can't get our birds a whole lot more accurate. So I'm personally looking at photographs of birds to get a new twist, a new animated look. I don't want something to look stereotyped, a decoy or a ceramic duck made in Japan. I think a carver like Pat Godin [of Brantford, Ontario] has done a terrific job in coming up with a bird in motion and movement. So I've done pieces like a black duck scratching its face. That's the direction we're heading in. That's why my aviary gives me the opportunity to see a duck doing something that you can put into a carving. I can walk to a window of this shop and look down and see that. And it can register in my mind whether I can really pull off that animated look. Perhaps it all starts here," Jim mused.

This was not my first introduction to aviaries. When I interviewed Jim for *How to Carve Wildfowl*, at his home in Annapolis, I was allowed to enter the fenced-in enclosure with its fiberglass pond to observe his ducks. For the same book, I had seen Larry Hayden's chainlink enclosure in Farmington Hills, Michigan, on an ice-chilled weekend in January of 1984.

Jim had known Hayden from such shows as the World Championships in Maryland and the U.S. National Decoy Show. Jim told me: "When I was building my first aviary, Larry told me that my carving would improve 30 percent. I didn't believe that was possible. But I've found, as people like Hayden and Foote did, that if you're exposed to ducks enough, something has to rub off. If you look at these birds day after day, feeding them, it's very, very helpful. Consequently, I'm constantly looking in the aviary to try to find an unusual pose or characteristic of that bird." He showed me a shoveler drake he had carved, its head bowed. "A shoveler, when in the water, has its bill ninety percent of the time sifting that water. So that's the way I carve it."

For Jim, though, the aviary has made other significant contributions to the success of his carvings. From

To Jim, the aviary is essential, not only to achieve the realism he strives for but also to capture an interesting or unusual pose. Here is a gadwall drake in a typical resting position.

A more elaborate carving is his black duck scratching its face. The photo for this was taken in his own aviary.

Jim's ducks are nearly tame enough for him to feed out of his hands. The oyster shells he is kneeling on keep the ground from turning to mud. On his left is a wooden cover that protects his photography hole. And in the foreground, left to right, are a pintail drake, a hooded merganser drake, and a black duck.

"Shooting through the nostrils" is how Jim describes the perfect profile shot. That achieved, he can then generate a head pattern from it. Notice the bit of light through this shoveler drake's bill.

them he has gotten patterns, profiles of side and top views from which all carvings begin.

Shooting Through the Nostrils

Most books about carving contain patterns. I always had assumed that they were casually done, almost freehand interpretations of that first step before the block of wood is carved. I thought, then, that bird patterns were no more than artistic interpretations, rough outlines that, hopefully with skill and luck, would end up looking like wildfowl. It was Jim's approach that corrected my thinking.

Before the advent of aviary photography, most carvers relied on photos taken in the wild or on community ponds. Today, using 35mm color slides and a 70 – 210mm macro zoom lens, Jim is able to go into the aviary and photograph the live birds. But a casually taken slide is not the strategy. To generate an accurate pattern, he must have what he describes as a perfect profile. How does he know when he has one? It is when he can look at the duck and see clearly through its nostrils. If the head is turned even ten degrees, the pattern will not be accurate, causing the head to be slightly smaller or larger in areas. Jim has called the perfect profile "a dead-on shot."

Once a slide is taken, it can be projected onto a wall-mounted piece of cardboard. Over that he will hold a piece of stiff white paper on which he draws the outline of the duck. But how does he know what size to enlarge the slide and consequently make the pattern?

Jim says this photo of a hooded merganser drake from his aviary will make a good head pattern. He points out the size and shape of the white in the head crest.

This gadwall drake will also produce a good head pattern, Jim says. He notes the way the head comes off the duck's neck and breast.

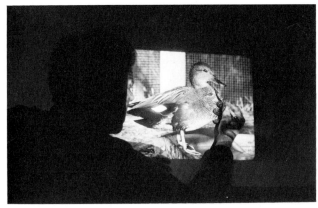

Jim will project a slide, as he does here with this gadwall drake, onto a piece of cardboard, enlarging or reducing its size according to the size of a study bill which he holds up against the image. He can then achieve an accurate pattern for the head, body, or both.

Yet another potential head pattern can be taken from this photo of a canvasback drake.

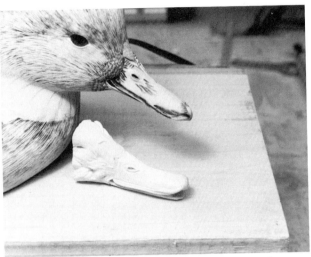

Crucial for determining pattern sizes is this study bill. Made of an epoxy compound and cast from a freshly killed or recently dead waterfowl to reduce shrinkage, this gadwall drake study bill was done by Bob Miller (see Appendix for address).

Demonstrating how he photographs his ducks, Jim sits in his aviary hole, which is forty inches deep.

Seen one morning through the window of the carving room of his shop are Jim's ducks. When the photo was taken, he had nineteen in the aviary, which he feels is too many.

Proportional References

I had assumed that Jim takes an overall measurement from a hand-held duck to get the right size for the patterns. Instead he relies on a popular aid called the study bill.

Probably originated by Bob Bolle of Roseville, Michigan (see Appendix for full address), a bill is cast from a freshly killed duck. A mounted bird's bill will shrink considerably due to its fleshy quality. Given this accurate cast, Jim will take from it what he calls a "proportional reference."

This measurement, which will affect all others on the pattern, is the length from the tip of the bill to the top corner of the upper mandible, or jaw. When he projects that perfect profile of his duck onto a screen, he can enlarge or reduce the image according to that length. He can then make the outline of the side profile of body and head.

And what of the top view? At one time, Jim had a braced platform of two-by-fours above the aviary to photograph directly above the ducks. Other photos were taken of hand-held ducks. But today he can actually shoot through a window in the shop. Once that slide is made and projected, it too can be enlarged or reduced given the size of the established side profile.

In-Ground Photography

Jim's Kent Island aviary is attached to and runs the length of his shop building, which serves as one side of the pen. Measuring 16x22 feet, surrounded by wire and posts, enclosed with wind-breaking plastic in the winter, its only outstanding feature (there is no coop or outbuilding here) is the pond. Concrete, the pond measures 8x13 feet, with a standpipe on one end to provide fresh water, and there's a drain at the bottom of its eighteen-inch depth.

Jim said the pond was designed after one he had seen in the National Zoo in Washington, D.C. Its gradually sloping slides make it easier for his diving ducks, with their legs so far to the rear of their bodies, to get in and out. A sharp lip, he pointed out, will actually wear the feathers off the breasts of these ducks.

At last count, Jim had nineteen birds in his aviary. There were five different types of hen and drake teal—green-winged, cinnamon, blue-winged, marble, and silver. Other ducks included a pintail, a shoveler, a black duck, a hooded merganser, a wood duck, a bufflehead, a canvasback, a ruddy duck and a gadwall.

Looking through a shop window, it won't take long to notice, between the outside fencing and the pond, a round wooden cover. What it hides from view is a pair of round cement sewer pipe-couplings, each thirty inches in diameter. Put together end to end, they provide forty inches of depth to allow Jim to sit in and literally photograph at nostril level.

Spooky Ducks

Is there any special reason for the size of the aviary? I asked. Jim responded, with some uncertainty, that it seemed the right size. "Some guys," he said, "make the mistake of building an aviary too big, to the point where the birds get spooky. The smaller the aviary is, however, without getting it ridiculously small, the friendlier and tamer the ducks get. But if they're wild and spooky, you don't get them in close for photographs. Running wild defeats the purpose of having the aviary." He also noted that some ducks, such as his canvasbacks and buffleheads, have become so tame that they can eat out of his hand.

Jim said it is advantageous to have others come to photograph his aviary birds. "The more people who come in with cameras, the tamer my birds get." I was not surprised, then, to see wildfowl painter Ned Ewell tucked down in the pipefitted ground of the aviary, taking photos of ducks that most likely would become watercolors in the near future.

Now I understand why Jim said, "Once you've had an aviary, it won't excite you to photograph wild birds two and three hundred yards away. The aviary spoils you."

Two Aviaries?

In spite of his success with his aviary, he still has some reservations about his present setup. "My aviary has too many birds in it," he said flatly. "This is my weakness. For some, it's liquor, for others it's chasing women. For me, I have to have ducks in the aviary." The problem here lies with a bird swimming in front of one he wants to photograph, something that happens frequently in his present aviary.

The ideal situation would be to have two aviaries, side by side. This way, he explained, "you can funnel two birds in, say a drake and hen canvasback, and photograph them extensively. And when you get the right shot, there's no chance of another bird swimming in front of the camera." Characteristic of Jim's

One of the problems with having too many ducks, Jim says, is that they get in the way of one another when photographing them. Here a black duck has interfered with getting a good study shot of a wood duck drake.

work ethic, he said, "That's down time." And an added bonus of the two-aviary setup is that the birds will become tamer.

Still, Jim felt his arrangement is superior to the first aviary he had. "There I had situated the aviary so I was always shooting into the sun. Now I have the sun and the bay behind me."

Black-and-White Ducks

Jim does not limit his photography to slides. He will also shoot black-and-white photos, using Kodak ASA 400 film. These kinds of shots, which can be easily filed and stored as contact sheets, can also provide unusual poses. And they are an aid to painting, giving Jim more contrast between colors than slides

Black and whites are used mainly for studying profiles and positions of ducks, and for determining the color values or contrasting colors. The latter can readily be seen on this pintail drake.

Jim is partial to teal. This one, a native to South America, is a silver teal he has in his aviary.

Jim points out that when a head is partially thrust forward, as this wood duck drake's is, it usually elongates the body.

This canvasback, Jim says, is in a semi-alerted position, one of many things he has learned since he started keeping his own ducks in 1976.

On this hooded merganser drake, note how the crest is lowered, while the tertials and tail are lowered in the water.

give. But whether he is shooting in black and white or color, he is constantly updating these references.

He advises anyone taking aviary photos, however, whether in color or black and white, to wait for a pose. "You just can't say to yourself that you have ten minutes to shoot the birds. I myself had tried that at the Annapolis aviary with poor results. I was too anxious to click off pictures of birds doing anything."

Rebellious Mallards

Are there any ducks that do not accept aviary life? Jim knew that answer immediately. "There's only one species of bird I wouldn't want again and that's a mallard. I had been told by several people that it's very difficult to keep these birds in your aviary because it's their nature to eat everything in sight and even kill to do it. I tried having a pair of mallards, one of which I

This photo of a relaxed black duck will lend itself to feather patterns and a study aid for the streaks in its face.

even raised from birth. But these two were so aggressive that one tried to kill a baby cinnamon teal. That's probably one of the reasons they're so prolific. You see mallards all over the world." He said Larry Hayden had a pair, "but I think they were segregated from the other ducks."

Generally, though, puddle and diving ducks will get along, Jim said, explaining that birds like shovelers and gadwalls are surface feeders, while diving ducks will descend into as much as thirty-five feet of water to get food. The puddle ducks, also called marsh ducks, are more likely to be found in marshes than in open water. They include ducks like mallards, black ducks, teal, wood ducks, pintails, widgeons. The divers are the canvasbacks, redheads, scaup, mergansers, eiders, scooters. Characteristic of diving ducks are bigger feet that are set farther back under their bodies, which, for some, make walking on land much harder.

Owing to the anatomy of the diving ducks, Jim puts out food for his waterfowl at the rounded edge of the concrete pond. "Some birds, when sifting the feed through their mandibles, will rotate their heads over the water and lose part of it. This is good for the diving ducks. They like to have the eighteen inches of water to dive in. That's why I leave the feed close to the water so they don't have to struggle to get at it."

Smart and Dumb Ducks

Jim has found what might be called an ambiguity about ducks. "They're pretty smart about having clean water. But they're stupid about defecating where they eat." Cleanliness, especially clean water, is a vital key to aviary maintenance, Jim told me. "I suppose the ideal situation is having clean, free-flowing water. One of my aviaries covered a five-acre beaver pond. But if you put an aviary right over a stream, you have a problem. You have to run wire below the surface because of the diving ducks.

"Here, I have my water pumped from a separate well, and I drain it every day. If the water is allowed to deteriorate, you'll actually see color changes in the feathers. A white breast will take on a dirty look, like a telltale ring around a collar. But if the water is clean, you won't have any trouble keeping the birds healthy."

Jim added that most of his birds like to have their photographs taken, and they will even perform if they have fresh water. "They'll splash around and preen and have a good time. So the best time to photograph

Jim places feed for his ducks on the rim of the cement pond. This allows for easy feeding by both diving and marsh ducks, the former having more difficulty walking on land because their legs are set far back under their bodies. In the water are a ruddy duck and canvasback, both diving ducks. The pintail drake, which is drinking, is a marsh duck.

them is actually when you give them that fresh water. You get some instant action."

Winter Problems

Another hygienic feature of Jim's aviary is its oyster shells scattered over the ground. Uncovered ground will turn to mud. But the shells prevent this from happening, and waste is washed down between the shells. In the winter, however, Jim puts down straw so the birds will not freeze to the shells. If that were to happen, feathers would be lost.

He recalled having a canvasback freeze to the wooden cover of his photography hole at his Annapolis aviary. "It was about zero degrees outside, and there was no straw on it. It was the one place that duck had decided to sit. But I somehow got him pried off without too many feathers being lost."

Winter offers another problem: the freezing of the pond water. To remedy this, Jim uses a stock-tank heater, designed to keep ice from livestock watering troughs. As Jim pointed out, some are submersible, some float. His is the floating type, which he has attached to a piece of Styrofoam, a kind of buoy.

Predators

I had seen nothing that looked much wilder than nocturnal rabbits that seemed set on outracing the

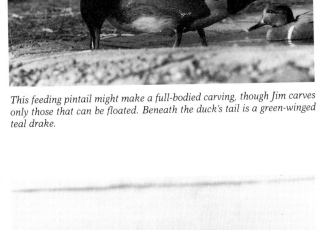

This feeding pintail might make a full-bodied carving, though Jim carves only those that can be floated. Beneath the duck's tail is a green-winged teal drake.

This black duck drake is displaying an unusual head position. It is a marsh duck that feeds in shallow water.

beams of my car's headlights. Jim would agree that predators are not really a threat to his ducks on Kent Island.

Still, he has surrounded his aviary with hardware cloth having one-half-inch mesh, noting that weasels, a problem at his upstate New York aviary and in other areas of the country, will get through mesh that has larger openings.

The top of the aviary is covered with wire mesh not only to keep the ducks in but also to keep predaceous owls out. "If a great horned owl could get into an aviary, it would take one or two birds a night," Jim said. "And if you trapped one off, two more will come in and try to take over the same territory."

Raccoons are also a threat to aviaries. To prevent them from getting in, Jim advised putting wire mesh down into the ground at least one foot. Less than that and the raccoons will tunnel under. He also suggested running the wire down and then parallel to the ground but away from the pen as an extra precaution. "I've been told by aviculturists that raccoons will even figure out how to unlock a hasp latch. So I use a spring-loaded latch.

"It's a real challenge having an aviary because of predators, cold water, keeping the pond clean. Even the drain may freeze."

Avian Personality

Jim will tell you that ducks are like people. "There are good-looking people and there are those not so fortunate. Aviculturists will tell you this, and it's one of the things I've learned since I've had aviaries. Even

This hooded merganser drake, a diving duck and a fish-eater, has a very alert look. Note the curvature of the tertials and how the tail lies flat in the water.

Jim thinks this hooded merganser drake might make an interesting carving for a full-bodied standing duck.

the coloring of the birds might be unexpectedly different. I remember one young bird, a cinnamon teal I hatched from a pair in my aviary. You'd think the bird would have the same color values [intensities of color] as its parents. But it didn't. So right there you can't tell me all birds of a species are exactly alike."

Another difference Jim had noticed in his aviary birds is in their personalities. He explained, "There are differences that are most pronounced during different times of the year. I think it has something to do with sex drives and desires. At one time during the year, the duck might be placid, at another, aggressive or even obnoxious. I've also noticed that some birds of the same species are friendlier than others." This, Jim believes, may have to do with imprinting, which is the behavior a duck learns immediately after birth based on a parent's instruction.

During my several weekends with Jim, I would take time from the photography and interviewing to look out at the ducks through the shop's windows. At times they would stand in stilt-leg sleeping postures; at other times they would actively engage in swimming and splashing water over their heads; at still others they would spend time watching me.

"Ducks pick up movement," Jim said during one of my observations. "I'm not sure they have such great distance vision, but they sure can pick up motion, which tips your hand if you're hunting."

Buying Ducks

I was curious to know how Jim got his aviary birds. Were they victims of hunting expeditions, wounded survivors brought to him in sacks? My belief was confirmed, I thought, by seeing a hunter friend of Jim's bring him a goldeneye that had been shot with only minor damage. It was an active addition to the aviary. But Jim had his doubts about how long it would stay alive, saying that a wild duck will not survive in an aviary. "It just won't go to the food provided." True to Jim's statement, the goldeneye died within four days of its arrival.

Where, then, does Jim get his ducks? Live birds, he told me, can be purchased through *Breeder's Gazette*, a magazine published in Salt Lake City, Utah. Jim described the publication as "the bible of breeders." He said it is not very difficult to purchase live birds, due to the demand from zoos and people with private collections of waterfowl. Yet he is fortunate, he remarked, in having a breeder of ducks near him in Grasonville, Maryland.

Prime Plumage

Is there an optimum time or age to buy an aviary bird? Jim said it should be done when the bird is at least in its second year of being raised in captivity, adding that it should be full-winged and not pinioned or disabled. Also, if a bird is purchased before September, the buyer will have the benefit of seeing the bird come into its best plumage during the fall and winter. "Molting birds aren't that attractive," he noted. "With younger birds, the problem is that you can have undeveloped feathers. It would then be like carving from a child instead of an adult model."

Jim says this photo offers a nice view of the way the pintail drake's tertial and scapular feathers droop over its body.

This is a ruddy duck drake in winter plumage.

Jim points out here the white horn or streak on the head and neck of this pintail drake.

This canvasback hen is in a relaxed position. The photo offers good details of its bill.

Jim would study a photo, such as this one of a swimming green-winged teal, for the vermiculation, or wavy lines, and the position of the duck's white sidebar.

Another photo offering a good study of vermiculation is this one of a wood duck drake.

Envelopes of Surprises

The first time I met Jim, I had noticed envelopes in his shop, the typical white business kind, collecting Foredom dust, strewn about on his carving bench and stacked near his painting table. What was in them were not bills but a wealth of references.

He has an envelope for every species of bird he carves, with a typical envelope containing head patterns, cardboard templates for primaries, tertials, and bills. He may even have some real primary feathers. And included will be notes pertaining to the last bird of the species he carved.

As complete a file of reference as this may seem, Jim has made a recent addition. It is a measurement from the center of the eye to a point on the back of the duck's bill. As you will learn later on, it's an important measurement when it comes to shaping the head.

What was the origin of these reference envelopes? Jim recalled that Michigan carver Jim Foote used a filing system for his photographs. "I guess I took this one step further to include other material. When I started carving, I knew I wouldn't be able to remember all the data about a bird, especially since I might not be carving a particular duck again for another six months or even a year. It made sense to save templates of feathers and tails so I didn't have to keep remaking them. This is something I pitch very strongly at seminars."

Jim related how, in the past, he would get his bill templates from freshly killed ducks he had hunted. Even today, pieces of paper with blood on them can be found in some of the envelopes.

More on Study Bills

But today, study bills have replaced bloodied templates. Used by most carvers, these bills have been cast in plaster material and epoxy resins to preserve the most minute details, from nostrils to wrinkles to the lamellae, which are the teethlike serrations of the mandibles—things photographs could never capture (see Appendix for suppliers). Jim told me these aids have become a carver's necessity.

The outer surface of a duck's bull is actually skin. This will dry out as soon as the duck is killed, resulting in the loss of moisture in it. In fact it even has a circulatory system. "This shrinkage was something I had to contend with years ago," Jim said. "Back then, we had to carve from mounted birds on which the bills were obviously incorrect. But I'd sort of guess and add a little here and there, but I think we all did that."

Study Skins

Jim has not only made bill templates in the field but has also brought home freshly killed birds. He will even do this today, though many that he needs as study aids are supplied by friendly hunters. And though at one time he would mount his own ducks, he finds a well-preserved skin just as valuable when it comes to painting. As evidence, study skins that look like victims of an avian executioner hang in a closet of his painting room.

Jim advised anyone who brings home a freshly killed duck to be used as a study aid to store it in a freezer. But still other precautions and preparations will add longevity to the duck. He suggested bringing newspaper into the field with packets of cotton. This material can be stuffed into the nostrils and throat of a duck. "This will absorb the blood and saliva that you don't want on those feathers, which you'll want as clean as possible for painting reference." With that done, the bird can be wrapped in newspaper, which will absorb any dampness on the feathers. Jim said that, once home, the bird should be rewrapped and the entire package put into a plastic bag.

I asked if bill shrinkage is the only problem with killed birds and how important are mounts as a source of reference. Jim answered that the latter have been useful when drawing feather groupings on a wooden bird and even to take feather measurements from. But primarily he sees the study skin as the best aid to painting. "A fresh mount kept under glass to keep the dust off will facilitate painting, but I still prefer to paint from a frozen bird."

Taxidermy Mistakes

I do not doubt that few, if any, carvers understand mounted birds and the problems with them as well as Jim does. "Having been a licensed taxidermist since I was sixteen, I can look at a mount and tell you what the problems are. The neck might be too long or too short. Even the head could come off the body wrong. Just because the head is attached to the body, the taxidermist is still relocating and positioning it with a Styrofoam or papier-mâché armature."

Though Jim feels many birds are incorrectly positioned and mounted by taxidermists, he believes this resting gadwall drake, done by Frank New-myer, is a good one (see Appendix for address).

I mentioned that many carvers use mounted birds when doing a decorative piece, such as a bird in flight. "Mounting for a pose is great," Jim responded, "but it goes back to whether the taxidermist is qualified. You can show him all kinds of photographs or drawings, but that doesn't mean he'll accurately mount the bird.

Even with accurately mounted birds, the skin will dry around the eyes and distort the look," he added. "And most carvers aren't knowledgeable enough to know if the look is correct. So invariably I'll see a carver make a mistake the taxidermist made."

Though Jim relied on two mounted birds when painting the gadwall (see Chapter 5), he said of the study skin, "I feel that if I can paint my carving as close to a fresh skin as possible, one I've kept dust-free, then I can defy anyone to tell me I haven't painted the right colors."

Attention and Retention

Coming almost circuitously back to his thinking about attention to details and how closely he studies live birds, Jim said, during our talk about skins and mounts: "Retention is very important. Someone like John Scheeler never seems to forget anything. I've known him to tell me about a carving I had done years ago. And people like Larry Hayden and Jim Foote look at a bird and just don't miss anything, or very little. Perhaps this is what separates the men from the boys.

"But people come to me and ask where their mistakes are, but they don't really want to know. They spend a lot of time on a piece, and they want to do better, but they don't want to hear the bad news. Still,

I think there are tactful ways to critique so you don't put yourself too much on the line. Hayden had a knack for critiquing a carving, so when he saw something wrong, he would say 'Check your reference.' It's a way of saying, 'you've got some problems in this area, so go look for them.' That's a good tactful way to criticize."

Jim recalled a doctor who would visit him and watch him work. "Not too seriously, I would ask him in the evening what he had learned for the day. One evening he said, 'J.D., attention to detail.' There's a lot to be said for that."

Pinups

Jim told me he is a strong believer in carving one species of duck at a time. "What I do is get all my references out, say on gadwalls, and have that ready in front of me, and I'll have photos of the bird on a corkboard. That way I can take the carving right over to the pictures as I work."

Jim is also reference-conscious to the point of saving not only photos but also a carved bird until another of the same species is started. "That way I have it for a reference. You can learn from the mistakes you've made if you have the previous bird there. If not, you won't remember things that didn't turn out as well as had been expected, or things you wanted to change. But after some years of carving, I'll more likely put notes into my reference envelopes of how I could do better."

This, and the following four photos of a gadwall drake, are typical pinups Jim keeps in front of him on a corkboard when carving. He says, when using a photo or even a mounted bird, that both primary groups must exist; those of many captive birds are missing. If they are, the tertials will not lay correctly on the bird. Photo by Larry Stevens (see Appendix for address).

Good aviary photos are important to the carver who can't have his own birds. What can be studied on this picture are the scapular feathers and feather groupings on the side pockets. Photo by Larry Stevens.

On this photo, Jim would study the transition between the breast pattern of white cups and vermiculation. Photo by Larry Stevens.

Still More References

The sources for reference material would seem to be inexhaustible to Jim. If an aviary is not feasible for a carver, he would suggest zoos that have waterfowl. There waterfowl can be observed and photographed. But like the many books on wildfowl alive and in wood, photographs are also coming onto the market as purchasable commodities. Some of the best I have seen, and included in this chapter, have been taken by Larry Stevens (see Appendix for address).

But Jim will always find his aviary his biggest asset. "An aviary is a real must. More and more questions are asked of me since people have learned that I have one. There's a lot of things to be gotten from live birds right on your own property."

Sawdust Ducks

There is yet another study aid, perhaps one that may become the easiest to obtain for the multitude of carvers doing waterfowl. It is the molded bird.

In my den roosts a ruddy duck, a molded though life-size reproduction of one Jim had carved in 1981. Prominent eyes look clearly out from the head. The small depressions in the bill are distinct. Feather groupings are accentuated while breast feathers are clearly raised in parallel rows. Every feather split has been reproduced, every quill line can be seen. Few admirers could tell that its origins are wood dust and not basswood.

Though Jim credits Randy Tull of Wisconsin with having supplied the first wooden duck carvings to be reproduced in synthetic materials as carving aids and

This relaxed pose shows the primaries, tertials, and scapulars. Photo by Larry Stevens.

Here the gadwall drake is preening. Photo by Larry Stevens.

This ruddy duck drake is composed of sawdust and glue, and is stained. It is a casting, or molded bird, done from one Jim had carved in 1981.

collectibles, Jim has packaged his own line of molded birds, most being sold through advertisements.

"I think they have a place because of the details that include textures, feather patterns, burning details," Jim said. Three of the six he has had molded are life-size. Patterns, then, can also be obtained as well as measurements of bills, heads, tails.

An interesting feature of these resin-made ducks is that they have the exact weights of their counterparts in wood. "That adds to the realism, and many people wouln't know they are molded unless you told them."

What these models are is a combination of sawdust mixed with a fine resin. In liquid form, the pecan wood dust and resin are poured into a rubber vulcanized mold at room temperature. "Not knowing it, you really are getting a wooden bird," Jim quipped.

Jim also explained that this gives a carving student an immediate bird to paint. "Obviously, before you can paint, you have to carve. With the molded bird, you can learn painting while mastering the carving. And you can repaint the bird fairly easily. These should be very helpful for my seminars."

3

The Gadwall:
A Carver's Challenge

The gadwall is one of 51 species of ducks and geese in the United States. Like many other birds, it makes that remarkably long migratory flight from the prairielands of Canada and the Dakotas. It can be found in all four of the flyways, those funneling corridors for wildfowl that run from northern to southern zones.

The impulse prompting bird migration, once thought to be a search for warmer weather, would seem to be the fact that birds must find enough food. Consequently, they seek areas with more hours of daylight, daring even the cold of Canada for longer food-gathering days.

Long northern flights are made, then, just before nesting, resisting what might be considered a temptation to stay in temperate zones in the southern latitudes. And though there is mortality among migrants, this movement has probably prevented extinction of most species that otherwise would not adapt to year-round conditions of a particular region.

Most gadwalls, when returning after nesting, head to Louisiana, where numbers have reached 1.5 mil-

lion. Some travel farther south to the Yucatan and Mexico. But only a few, taking a peculiar detour from the Mississippi flyway, journey to the Chesapeake. Perhaps no more than a thousand winter there.

Jim has seen some near his home, but he has observed more when he hunted on the St. Lawrence. The gadwall, despite the large population figures given, is not the most abundant duck in North America; the most common is the mallard. It does not have the striking, almost gaudy colors of a wood duck. It lacks the recognizability and history of the canvasback, fashioned of reeds and feathers by an American Indian one thousand years ago and found preserved in a Nevada cave. What, then, is the appeal of the gadwall, and why did Jim choose it as the focal project for this book?

Jim explained: "Gadwalls are not like mallards, which everyone sees and relates to immediately because we know what they are. That's one of the challenges for the carver. But [with the gadwall] you've also got blending of colors with light feather edges that merge into vermiculation. And anytime you've

One of the aspects Jim finds intriguing about the gadwall is the head with its short bill, blocky shape, and pattern of streaks.

It is a challenge to take on a gadwall due to its coloration and markings as well as its unfamiliarity to many carvers.

got a bird with a head pattern that has fine streaks or markings, those things make the bird real interesting. So I'd say it has the kind of detail in carving and painting that separates your carved bird from the next guy's."

Jim's reasoning is also esthetically grounded. "To me, a gadwall, also called a gray duck, is a very beautiful bird, with soft colors." He also noted that it has a definite profile, different from that of other ducks. "It has a sharp crown, and an adult drake will have something of a comb on the back of the head."

Jim said that very few gadwalls show up in competitions. "In fact," he said, "there are a lot of people who

can't even identify them." Still, he has seen a number of them near Chincoteague, Virginia and Assateague, Maryland.

Getting Started

It was an overcast morning when the gadwall was begun. Jim was up at seven and had fed the ducks and Teal and made me breakfast, and we were out in the shop on schedule--at 8 a.m.

Most of the work would be done on the pressed-wood benchtop in the carving room. Above it are hung tools and grinding bits with a small shelf for a

Jim's carving room, which measures only 12 x 15 feet, is more than adequate to accommodate three sizable workbenches and a bandsaw.

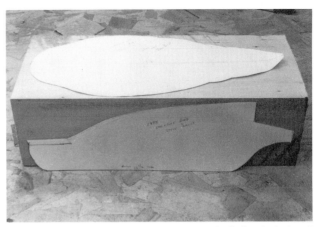

Two paper patterns begin the gadwall drake, the body of which will measure 13½ inches. These are for a bird with its head thrust forward, giving it an elongated shape. It was commissioned by Steve Davis of High Point, North Carolina, one of nearly thirty birds Jim carves each year.

radio. At that bench, on a barstool, Jim would shape, burn, and texture the gadwall until it was ready to move into the smaller painting room.

The carving room is also large enough for a bandsaw and two other workbenches, one with a drill press, a sanding machine, and dusty wooden patterns, the other covered with birds carved and mounted, books, and a bus box of water. Yet, when Jim needs something, few steps are required, so there is little effort wasted in reaching for a tool or pattern. There is a compactness to this 12x15-foot room, a means of efficiency perhaps more apparent in the specialized painting room.

Sometime in the past, Jim projected a slide of a gadwall, the head perfectly profiled, with perhaps a touch of blue water showing through the nostril holes. With the study bill providing the critical measurement, the body was brought into focus, probably reduced in size, a pattern was traced and filed away for a day when a gadwall would be carved for a competition, or a book. But whatever the case, the patterns were ready for use that day, labeled as to species and sex. I remembered what Jim had told me when I interviewed him for *How to Carve Wildfowl:* "Your carving is no stronger than your reference material."

Jim had cut the block to size the night before and had the cardboard patterns for the head, side, and top profiles on the carving bench. My first photos were of the patterns resting against and on top of the block, and I recall wondering how long it would take before a duck emerged, complete with feathers, eyes, and paint.

Before Jim traced around the patterns, he told me about a trick he had learned from his carver friend

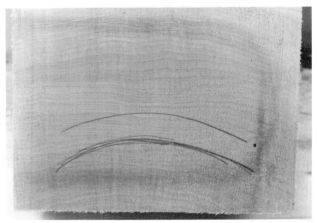

Before he begins, Jim makes sure the wood grain will be curving with the body of the bird, i.e., the growth rings will be arcing in conjunction with the top of the body. This gives more stability when undercutting tertials and tail feathers later on.

Ken Harris. He checks the end grain of the block to determine in what direction the growth rings (a reminder that this material was once alive) are curving. This is necessary to know for a later stage in carving: shaping the tail and tertials, the feathers that lie in the rear of the duck. "I don't use inserts or separate pieces of wood for those feathers," he said. "And since I don't, if the grain is not running convexly or arcing downward with the shape or flow of the feathers around the body, there's less stability in these thin areas. So the end grain has to run with the slight curvature of the feathers. Otherwise it would only weaken them."

Jim also said, before he thumbtacked the patterns to the block and began outlining them, that this would be an interesting carving because the head would be thrust forward. "It gives more of an elongated body pattern that might indicate swimming or feeding." And characteristic of his axiomatic references, he added, "But those are things you see in the aviary. I guess they're basic to all ducks, whether gadwall or teal. Yet, it's incorporating things like this in the carving that achieves the realism I want."

Patterns and Plugs

As he lined up the top and side patterns on the block with the aid of a square and miter and pencil

line, he noted that he would leave a little extra wood around the perimeters of the top and side patterns. He explained, "I leave a space so I can save a top section of the block that will be used as a pattern for future carvings. It's better to trace around a rigid piece of wood rather than a flexible piece of cardboard or paper. It's also a cross-reference and a permanent one if the paper ones are ever lost or destroyed."

But there is yet another and perhaps unique use for the top wood profile that I learned about later that day. Since many of Jim's birds are hollowed to float, that waste piece can be a convenient and correct-size plug that would cap the bottom of the bird after wood

The block for the gadwall is 14 x 6½ x 4½ inches. The steel square and miter is used to line up the top and side patterns.

Patterns are thumbtacked to prevent them from moving when being traced.

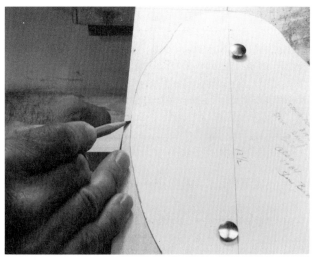

Space is left so that when the top and side views are cut away, they can be saved as wooden patterns for future reference. Also, notations of changes can be written on them.

A little extra space is left at the tail area before bandsawing to prevent the tail from coming out short when it is being carved.

is removed from the interior. "This wood should be anywhere from one-quarter- to three-eighths-inch thick, a comfortable size for a body plug," he said.

There was one more concern before the block was ready to be taken to the bandsaw. When drawing the profiles, Jim was especially careful to leave at least an extra inch of wood where the tail comes to a point. So rather than cutting the tail to the exact shape of the profile, Jim will cut it to the end of the block. "It's too easy when carving," he said as he drew a small arrow at the end of the block, "to end up too short on the length of the tail. And since this is such a thin area, I'm not really having to cut away a lot of extra wood if I'm on the long side."

Squaring the Block

The tablesaw in the storage area that adjoins the carving and painting rooms accomplishes the cutting to size of his bulky planks of basswood, both ripping the pieces lengthwise for thickness and crosscutting them for length. But it is the six-inch jointer, a machine found in most cabinetmaking shops, that is used for squaring the edges of the wood so that they meet at right angles.

"If the block weren't square," Jim said, "or reasonably square, the bird, when cut out with the bandsaw, would have one side higher than the other." And this, he said, would make for a lopsided duck, or require extra carving to bring down one side.

Shaping with the Bandsaw

The thirteen-inch throat of Jim's Rockwell bandsaw is sizable enough to accommodate almost any duck as its squarish body is pushed through its blade. And indeed, the gadwall block moved easily across the table of the machine. After the waste wood of the side profile was removed, he nailed the top portion back on with finishing nails, and ran the blade along the pencil lines of the top profile. When finished, the body was still squarish, but the shape of a duck was present. But Jim had not finished bandsawing. Tilting the adjustable top to its full forty-five-degree angle, Jim again put the block to the blade and started removing the sharp corners. The skip-toothed blade in the machine acts like a rasp, shaping the block. "The more done with the bandsaw, the less shaping required with the grinding tools," Jim said above the rotary hum of the saw as it made faceted cuts along the edges of the gadwall.

But the bandsawing was still not finished until the head was partially shaped. Here he had drawn only the side profile on the head block, and when he bandsawed it, he did no shaping. That would be done later, with the use of grinding tools, after he had decided on the size of the bill.

The Linden Tree

I stated earlier that Jim's primary wood is basswood. I was familiar with it early in my own cabinet-

Jim's thirteen-inch-throat Rockwell bandsaw cuts the side view to shape first.

Since the top view was cut away during the previous step, it must be nailed back on before the block goes back into the bandsaw.

The top profile is now cut to shape. Interestingly, this leaves not only a wooden pattern for the top view, but also a possible wooden plug, which will seal the bottom of the bird after it is hollowed. Hollowing of decorative decoys is a requirement for many competitions.

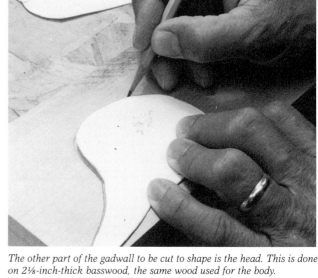

The other part of the gadwall to be cut to shape is the head. This is done on 2⅛-inch-thick basswood, the same wood used for the body.

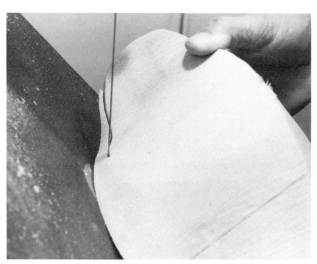

A skip-tooth blade removes sharp corners.

This too is bandsawed to shape, though only the side profile is done.

The same blade also acts as a rasp, making facets while the tabletop of the bandsaw is tilted to its maximum forty-five degrees.

making career. Like many people I knew making furniture, I took a turn at relief carving, even doing a decorative, high-relief eagle or two. My lumber dealer told me that most of the carvers he knew were using basswood. And though I later turned to other woods such as walnut and mahogany to carve, I found that basswood did work well with sharp tools. And once I decided to paint my eagles, the wood took enamels and acrylics well.

Basswood is really the linden tree, though abroad it is called whitewood and lime. It is not uncommon in this country and Canada. With low-growing branches, it was once favored as a shade or ornamental tree. It is light in color, with a whitish wood and a creamy white to pale brown sapwood, the central portion of the tree. In terms of weight, it is relatively light: only about 26 pounds per cubic foot (oak is nearly double that).

There is little warping and cracking as the wood dries, so large pieces can be utilized. And the cell structure is extremely close, making it an excellent base for paint. These are good reasons why it has been used here and in Europe by woodcarvers long before Jim and I were born.

Tupelo Gum

Despite the definite advantages of basswood, there is another wood favored by carvers such as Tan Brunet and John Scheeler. It is tupelo gum, also called water tupelo, a relatively new wood for carvers. It is neither an ornamental tree nor a shade tree, for it is found in swamps. In fact, Louisiana swamps have produced World Championship pieces, such as a pair of redheads by Brunet, and the goshawk and crow sculpture by Scheeler.

It was Scheeler who generously gave me a large flitch of tupelo gum he had received from friends in Louisiana when I interviewed him for *How to Carve Wildfowl*. I had told him about an ornamental armoire I was reproducing, with a large carving applied that was the focal point of the two-door cabinet with reliefed birds as its motif. It was only the keenest blade, I found, that could slice away the wood. A dull tool would only push into what seemed like a rubbery material. It was then that I decided to try a Dremel Moto Tool and bits and got far better results.

It is really only the bole or first few feet of the tupelo gum tree, one that can grow some four feet in diameter and seventy feet high, that is taken from the swamps. It is usually chainsawed at low tide, to get the wood that is softer due to the dampness and lack of sunlight. And, because of its damp habitat, it has the unnatural ability to be carved while still wet or unseasoned and can be dried without serious cracking. Also, it can be carved from sizable flitches or blocks without the same stress checks as the wood dries.

As a medium for paint, many carvers find it unequaled. It can actually take paints without a primer, owing to its color and density. And it can be sanded nearly paper-thin without losing any appreciable strength.

Basswood Preferred

Still, during my visits to many of the top wildfowl carvers in this country, I found that basswood was favored over tupelo by the majority. Like tupelo, basswood has little grain to be seen and to cause a knife to stray and tear away delicate pieces. And, like tupelo, its light color and consistent texture make it easy to cover with paint, without highlights and dark splotches.

Jim agrees with all of these assessments. But there are, he said, two distinct types of the wood: a highland and a lowland variety. The highland he described as having a yellowish color, "almost maple in appearance, and found at higher elevations. Quite frankly, I prefer that to the lowland bass, which is much whiter and fuzzes so much more. That makes it harder to deal with when sanding." But though Jim claimed the highland basswood is harder to work, "all you really need is a sharp knife or chisel."

He went on to say that the only place he might want a softer piece of bass would be for the head. "It's where I might like to try tupelo. In a softer wood, you can twist the burning pen a little easier, which is one of my techniques."

Jim admitted to having tried tupelo gum, and, as I discovered later, he in fact used it for his gadwall's inserted primary feathers and for the body of a cinnamon teal drake. "But basswood's awfully hard to beat, even having played around with tupelo, which doesn't seem to carve quite as well. The only other advantage I see is that tupelo stones better when you go against the grain, that is, it doesn't fuzz up.

"Interestingly, I've found carvers who have used tupelo all their lives suddenly looking for a good piece of basswood. Maybe it's a case of things looking greener on the other side of the fence. To me, I guess, there are good pieces of tupelo and good pieces of basswood. But a lot goes back to what I got used to. I learned with bass and stayed with it. I even brought mine from upstate New York before I moved to Maryland. I had the better pieces culled out for me at a lumberyard there."

Another carver I had interviewed for *How to Carve Wildfowl* was Ernest Muehlmatt, who uses only jelutong, a wood brought here from Malaysia. Had Jim tried it? "I haven't used jelutong enough to really comment on it," he answered, "but it seemed to have pith marks or pockets." But one of the finest heads he had done, one of a baikal teal, was carved from jelutong.

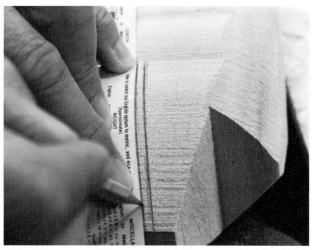

Before Jim starts roughing out the bird, he lays out the tail, which is angled up. The distance between the lines is only three-sixteenths of an inch.

Calipers determine the exact height of the tail on the bird's side.

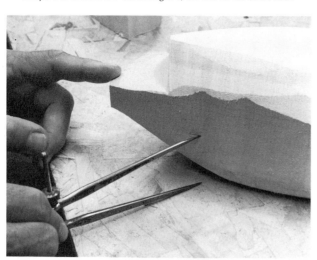

These same calipers assure the same height on the opposite side.

"I think it's human nature to look for what the other guy has," Jim commented. "I think it's the same with tools. When I teach seminars, I see people using basically the same tools I'm using, seeming to think that because I have a certain tool, that's what makes the carving good. But it's really the man or woman using it."

But Jim warned that even though the grain is nearly invisible with basswood, grain changes do occur. And unless a tool moves or turns direction to compensate for those changes, splitting can occasionally result.

Hogging off Wood

Unlike most carvers, who immediately go to the Foredom to start shaping the bird after the bandsaw is shut down, Jim goes to a Dumore die grinder (see Appendix for address of manufacturer, Electric & Tool Service Co.) Unlike the Foredom, the motor of this tool is in the handpiece instead of a hanging cannister. But more unlike the Foredom, his Dumore removes wood in a fury of wood dust that forced me to take refuge in his paint room when he used it.

Jim explained, literally after the dust had settled, that the grinder both runs at a higher rate of speed and removes wood more quickly than the Foredom. The major purpose for using it, he said, "is to hog off wood." He can hold it in one hand, the body of a duck in the other, and round off edges that remain after bandsawing, putting in indentations for the wings, working underneath the rump area.

As he worked with the tool on the rump, he said, machine temporarily turned off, that on a gadwall, the

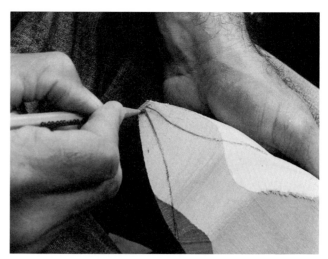

Jim then lays out the portion underneath the rump with pencil.

undertail portion extends all the way to the tips of the tail feathers, whereas on some ducks it might end an inch or more back from the tips of the tail feathers. Jim reminded me that "this again comes from knowing our bird, either from a good mount or from aviary photos."

He wore a hat and mask for this work, and had a sizable cone-shaped carbide bit in the machine. There was another explosion of wood dust as the bit ground off more basswood.

He did, however, switch to the Foredom with a rotary rasp attachment to achieve a more defined cut underneath the tail.

I asked Jim about the safe use of these tools when he had finished using the two grinders. He said, "It's very easy to catch a bit in your shirt because you're working so close to your body to steady your arms, especially with the die grinder. And there's a real tendency for the bit to slide off the wood. But you learn very quickly what the rotating bit is going to do, in terms of it walking away on you or spinning around an edge." He advises carvers to work alone, recalling that "the only time I cut myself was when someone who was watching was in a hurry to leave, and so I was in a hurry with the carving."

He pointed out that Foredom bits do not survive in the die grinder. They have a tendency to come apart owing to the Dumore's greater speed.

Head Left and Side Pockets

Jim set the wood body on his workbench, amid a thick layer of sawdust. He took the gadwall head, with

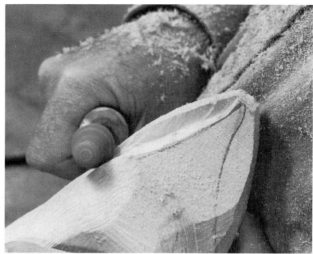

With the Dumore and carbide burr, wood is relieved or reduced from around the tail and rump.

A three-quarter-inch diameter rasp and Foredom refine the previous shaping.

He starts to shape the body with a die grinder called a Dumore (see Appendix under Electric & Tool Service Co. for address) and a cone-shaped, three-quarter-inch burr made of carbide steel. He describes this as "hogging off wood."

Shown here are the few cutters, plus a cloth sanding wheel, that Jim uses throughout the shaping of a duck.

It is back to the carbide burr and Dumore to define a duck's side pockets.

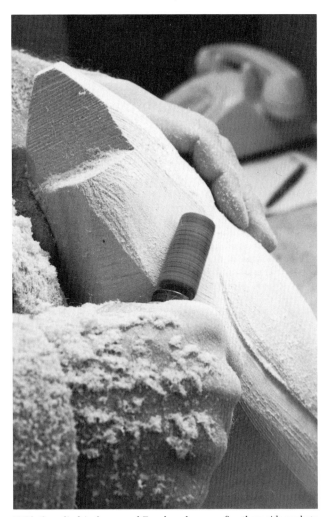

With the cylindrical rasp and Foredom, he can refine these side pockets. The advantage of using this tool and bit is that they do not remove wood too fast.

only its side profile defining it, and set it on the small shelf left at the front of the body. "It's time," Jim said, "to determine which way the head will lie on the body, whether it's going to be turned left, right, or straight ahead." But the straight-ahead look is not a common pose for his ducks. "I just try to stay away from anything stereotyped or stiff or that has that old-fashioned decoy look," something he has avoided since his first gunning decoys.

But other characteristics of the bird must coincide with a turned head. Jim told me this could be better explained when he painted, but he did say that when he decided to have the head facing to his left, he would also have the left wing dropped downward slightly to reveal the bird's coverts. "This reveals some color that wouldn't ordinarily be seen. So what is happening is that a left-turned head will, in most cases, get people to look at the bird's left side. And the color that will be revealed is a touch of rust, a small bonus in the overall color sheme."

So an arrow was drawn on that shelf, indicating the turn of the head and which side would require more wood to be removed from the front of the body.

Before Jim went on to another machine, he held a pencil against the rear of the bird, angled against the rounded flank. "These are side pockets that have a sloping angle. I hate to look at the rear of a duck and see a boxcar look. I can recognize this because, for the first few years of carving, I was not getting this curvature," he admitted. "It's important because this is one of the key things to getting the bird looking the way it

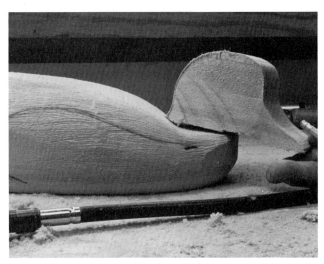

At an early point in the carving, Jim will determine at what angle the head will come off the body. The major effect, aside from getting away from a stiff pose, is on the painting of the bird.

Jim will reveal more color on the side of the bird that its head is turned to. Here the white of the speculum is revealed on this side since the turn of the head should cause people to look there.

should look. I guess it's what you call 'carving in the round.'"

Drum Sanding

Jim described sanding as "something I've never gotten very excited about. So if I can find anything to make that process go quicker, I'll use it." At this stage it was necessary to refine the Dumore and Foredom work already done. And like the grinding, Jim found the biggest and fastest tool possible. What does a great deal of finish-type sanding is the pneumatic sanding

With a pencil, Jim illustrates the forty-five degree angle he tries to achieve between the side pockets and tertials.

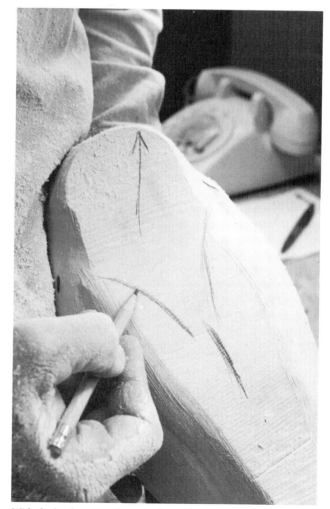

With the head position determined as indicated by the arrow, his next step is to pencil in the shoulder area.

The rasp used in previous steps now shapes the shoulders, leaving a sharp cut.

This photo shows the body partially shaped with the side pockets and shoulder area defined.

Jim uses a pneumatic drum sander for clearing away the marks left by the rotary bits and attachments. The drum measures three inches in diameter and nine inches in length.

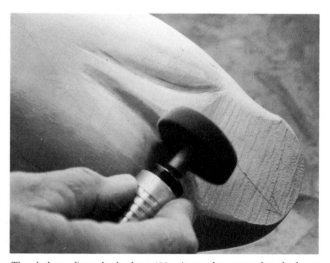

The cloth sanding wheel, about 100 grit, reaches areas that the larger drum sander cannot.

Finally, hand-sanding is done with a 100-grit cloth-backed paper.

drum he has bolted to the bench on the wall that faces the aviary.

The drum, some three inches in diameter and nine inches long, with a 120 grit sleeve, does a remarkably fine job on the basswood. With its ¾ horsepower motor, it seemed as quick and efficient as his Dumore. But some areas behind the head and those small depressions where the wings join the body could not be reached with the sleeve. For these Jim used the Foredom and a 100-grit sanding wheel. And finally, and only when absolutely necessary, Jim used the traditional hand-sanding method, with a cloth-backed paper. Made in Switzerland and introduced to him by John Scheeler, he said it is the best sanding cloth he has ever used.

Setting the Tempo

Sanding to Jim is the busy work of carving. But on the positive side, it may well be one of the most important steps in achieving a fine bird. "It sets the pace and tempo for later steps," Jim said. And what are they?

"When you burn details into wood that is not sanded properly, and paint is applied over that, you end up with a lot of residue that is highlighted by the paint. You don't really notice it or see it until that paint is applied. Also, without proper sanding, the grain may show through, even with basswood." Putting it another way, Jim said, "One way to see the flaws in your carving is to put a coat of gesso [a primer] on the bird. It will show you immediately where you come up short, particularly in those areas not sanded well."

Hollowing

Finished with the top of the progressing gadwall for the time being, Jim went to work on the bottom—not to finish but to hollow it. "I spend a lot of time hollowing these birds out," he said as he scribed a line around the flat bottom, perhaps one-half inch in from the perimeter. "The lighter my bird is, the better it seems to ride in the water." As he continued the pencil line, using only his fingers as a guide, he added, "I hate to see a carving ride real low in the water. It's a pet peeve you discover when you're judging. You pick up the carving only to find that it's solid, that it has so much extra weight to it. It seems to take away from the bird. Contestwise, it's where balance and riding ability are important."

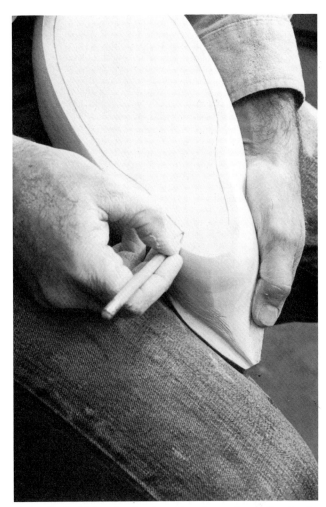

This gadwall will be a floating decorative piece and must therefore be hollowed. To do this, Jim will first lay out a line on the underside of the body approximately one-half inch from the outside edge.

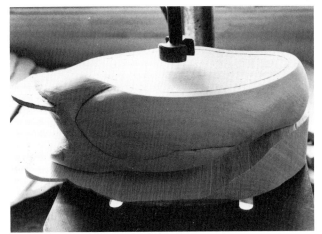

This is the body for the cinnamon teal drake, made from tupelo gum, that is also being worked on. What remains of the top view forms a cradle, not only to keep the bird from rocking as it is hollowed but also to keep the drill press table from marring the wood.

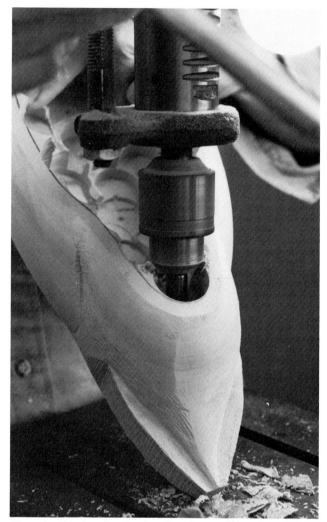

Back to the gadwall, Jim starts at the tail area, using a 1¼-inch Forstner bit to remove wood. The depth of the cut has to be determined before-hand to prevent the bit from going through the bird. Note how the scrap wood is wedged underneath the bird.

Using his body for leverage, Jim works the bit around the perimeter.

The gadwall is then tipped on its tail so that wood from the inner rump area can be removed.

He will, then, spend some two to three hours hollowing a bird as he did with the gadwall. Once this outline was made, which not only keeps him from breaking through the sides but also provides a rim onto which he would fit a plug, he went to the drill press, located next to the sanding drum. A Forstner bit was in the drill chuck. This bit, I knew from my own woodworking, provides an advantage over others in that it creates a round but flat-bottomed hole. It does not clog, it is unaffected by knots or changes in grain direction, and overlapping holes are easily achieved. It is, then, ideal for hollowing a wooden bird.

Working from the back, Jim made a series of holes around the perimeter, being careful not to overstep the plug line he had drawn and equally careful to set the depth gauge of the drill so that the bit would not break through the bird. He propped a waste piece of wood, one cut away from the bird's side with the bandsaw, under the rounded portion of the duck to help steady it on the metal table of the machine. It seemed a good fit, for he kept it there as he worked the bird around in a complete circle, the overlapping bit penetrations taking out more and more wood. Finally, he stood the bird on its tail end and bored into the cavity that could not be reached without breaking through the body.

The next phase of hollowing was done with a hand-tool, a small carver's gouge. With this, he cleaned up the concave notches left in the walls by the Forstner bit. With that completed, he brought out the Foredom and the rotary rasp he had used on the outside rump and beveled a forty-five-degree angle on the lip of the cavity. This bevel would later accept a wood plug with a matching bevel, he explained. For a final cleanup,

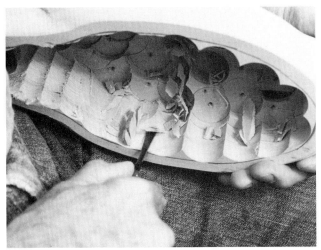

A small gouge cleans up the inner walls of the duck. Jim tries to lighten up the bird as much as possible, saying that the lighter it is, the easier it is to balance for proper flotation in the water.

The Dumore die grinder and a three-quarter-inch-diameter steel cutter, rotating at 34,000 rpm, remove even more wood. Also, the cutter's roundness is excellent for the inner sides.

The lip of the hollowed bird is beveled at approximately forty-five degrees to accept a bottom plug.

the die grinder, this time with a ball-shaped cutter, worked the inside walls of the bird, removing even more wood that the Forstner and gouge could not. Then Jim was ready to balance and enclose the bird.

Plugging the Bird

Jim put a stiff piece of paper over the bottom of the bird and penciled the outline of the outer edge of the bevel. This would be the pattern for the plug. And though he could have used the scrap left when the gadwall was bandsawed earlier, Jim preferred to take a fresh piece of half-inch-thick basswood, draw a line around the pattern he had cut out, and bandsaw that

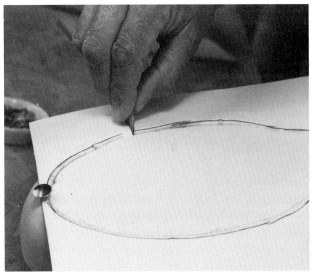

Jim now establishes the plug pattern with a piece of paper and pencil.

The pattern from the last step is transferred to a three-eighths-inch-thick piece of basswood, though he could have used the top-view scrap wood.

This photo shows the angle of the plug and interior body lips.

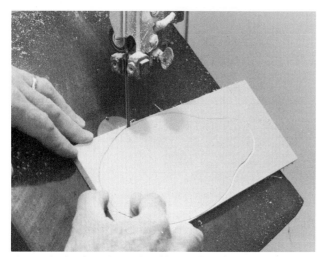

The wood is bandsawed with the table tipped to a forty-five-degree angle so that the bevels match.

to shape. He cut it with the bandsaw table tilted to its maximum of forty-five degrees. This would make the bevel to fit the one he had rasped out of the bottom of the gadwall.

Does he nail this plug to the bird? Jim does not use nails but a two-part epoxy called Tuf-fil to join the two pieces of wood, a material that Jim described as a kind of fiberglass, which would also keep the duck watertight.

But staying afloat is only part of the strategy behind making waterfowl to be entered in the floating competitions. Having them well balanced is another, and there are judges at these contests who poke the birds with rubber-tipped sticks to test how they ride in the indoor waters.

Lead weights are what Jim uses to balance a bird

that may well have had a bit too much wood removed from one side or the other, making the bird tilt or list. Yet, if the bird is plugged and sealed, how can he make the corrections with the weights?

Jim's strategy is not unique, but perhaps his materials are. He will first and simply clamp plug and bird together with a rubber band. Then he floats the assembly on a thin sheet of plastic, dry-cleaning variety, laid over a waterfilled bus box. Jim had seen other carvers wrap their birds in Saran Wrap, some even dunking an unprotected bird into water. But Jim's method enables him to easily and quickly remove the dry plug, make the corrections by placing pieces of lead on the inside of the bottom, and replace the bird on the floating plastic. So thin is this material, it has little effect on the natural buoyancy of the bird.

With weights secured in place, the plug can then be firmly sealed with epoxy. But the joining is not a haphazard effort, and any possible crack in the sealer is well covered. Jim has seen some fine decorative waterfowl that took water into their cavities. "Even a little moisture in the bird can cause the bottom to

Here the gadwall, farther along in details, is tested in a bus box of water to see how well it is balanced. Covering the water is very thin dry-cleaning plastic. This keeps the duck dry and presents little interference between bird and water.

spring a leak," he explained, though he could not recall having seen a plug detach. "But when a duck is in a tank of water sometimes three or four hours, you'd better make sure that bottom is watertight."

Full-Bodied Ducks

Yet not all of Jim's floating waterfowl have flat bottoms. He will carve some that he describes as full-bodied ducks, ones slightly rounded on their bottoms and made to rest on walnut bases. Held this way, it is no problem to put entire webbed feet on a bird.

To make a full-bodied duck, Jim uses two pieces of wood instead of the one-piece construction. These he sandwiches together with the upper piece being one-and-one-half times thicker than the bottom. But the top board, which comprises two-thirds of the volume, is hollowed while the lower wood is left solid. "I want as much weight as I can get on the bottom for stability in the water," Jim explained.

Bigger or Smaller?

I cannot recall what triggered my question about the size of a duck. I do know that I had read an interview with a carver who said he made his ducks a bit larger, perhaps healthier, than might be expected for

Small pieces of lead are added to the inside surface of the plug to counter any listing of the bird. Notice that the lead is placed on the side opposite the direction the head will turn.

competitions. I related that to Jim as he shifted the small pieces of lead around on the plug. He did not have to think about a response, for he had a theory of his own about how to present a bird to judges. It was not what I had expected him to say. "I go for a smaller bird. Why? Because a smaller bird projects better, attracts more eyes, especially in a tank, than something oversized. It's only a theory, but having won some

Not all of Jim's floating decorative birds are flat-bottomed. This gadwall is made from two pieces of basswood sandwiched together, with the top half hollowed. He calls this a full-bodied bird.

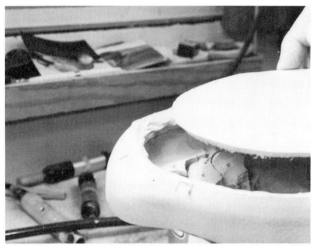

Jim uses Freeman Tuf-fil, a repair and building material similar to fiberglass, to seal the plug to the body. It must be thoroughly sealed so water cannot enter.

competitions, I can't believe my theory is too far astray."

He elaborated: "If you have ten green-winged teal in a tank, and they're fairly equal in size, it's the smaller bird that wins. It seems to reach up and grab you. But don't get me wrong. You can't have something small that's poorly carved and expect to win with it."

He also said that he made his birds looking up when he could. "They're perkier, that's why. And when I'm displaying at a sales table, the higher up off the table I can get the birds, the better. Almost eyeball-to-eyeball if that's possible."

He remembered judging floating birds one year and had seen a well-carved widgeon in the tank. But it had its head down in the water. Jim shook his head negatively. "It just looked sickly."

4

From Mandibles
to Primaries

Getting a Head

When Jim got out a reference envelope penned GADWALL and emptied its contents of feathers, real and wood, bill template, and drawings on pocket notebook paper, he described yet another appeal of the gadwall.

"I think a gadwall head is one of the prettiest heads of any duck, not only because of its coloration but also because of its design." And pointing to the head profile he had used earlier, he said, "That head has a distinct profile, with a shape I think is different from any other duck's. It has an almost subtle crest to it, and with a square, blocky look. Another unique thing is what's going on directly behind the bill. There's a pronounced depression there, more so than any other head I've examined. It's almost pinched in."

He turned from his bench and reached to a shelf to bring down what was unmistakably a gadwall head, a dusty and silent observer for what might have been years. I assumed the basswood head, burned and well detailed, had been done by Jim. I was mistaken.

"Every time I carve a gadwall, I take this out for reference," he said. "It was carved by John Scheeler. And if you notice, John made that depression behind the bill. It's something that a lot of judges don't even notice."

Jim put the head aside and picked up a bill template. This would be the first step in establishing the top profile. This paper pattern was not one he had gotten from a study bill but from a live bird. He had traced it while one of his daughters held the gadwall in her hands. A centerline down the middle of the still-blocky head helped him locate the template and draw an outline.

But Jim was not satisfied with the paper pattern alone. From another shelf he took a study bill of a gadwall drake and took a pair of calipers from his tool board. "There are two critical measurements here," Jim explained. "One is from the bottom of the V, which is where the bill and forehead meet, to the very tip of the bill. And the other is the width at the top of the V." He reflected a moment and said, "It's not really a V, though."

"An ogee curve?" I suggested, explaining that it is a

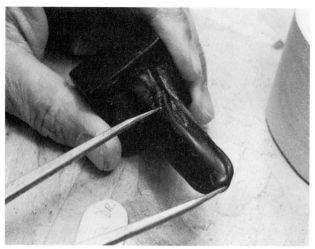

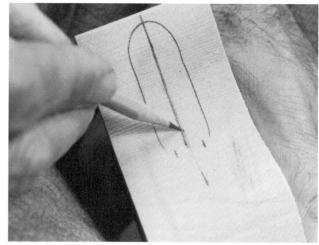

Many of the early work stages will be done on the head. Only when that is finished will he go back to the body. The bill is probably the most difficult part of the head, and requires the use of a study bill for details and accuracy. This one was made by Bob Bolle (see Appendix for address). Here Jim begins by taking a measurement from the tip of the bill to the lower point on the back of the bill, the sides of which have been described as a pair of ogee curves.

Here the pencil points to a mark that indicates the junction of the ogee curves. Note the centerline and the two short lines. The distance between them is a measurement taken from the top of the study bill's ogee curves.

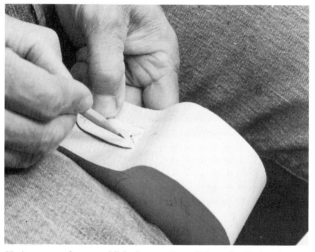

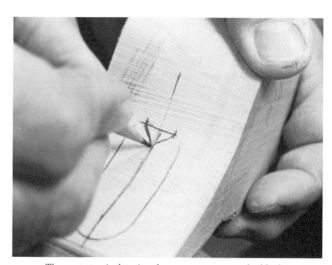

He is now ready to establish the top view of the gadwall's head on the block of wood. To get this, he has used not only the calibrated measurement of the last step but also a paper pattern drawn from a handheld live duck.

The next step is drawing the ogee curves onto the block.

curve that reverses itself, one I had learned about in cabinet work and found as the profile of many moldings. Jim agreed that it was such a curve, noticeably pleased by my observation as he carefully sketched out the ogee curve at the rear of the gadwall bill.

When completed, most of the tools and bits used to shape the body were put back into action. The bandsaw again cut the top profile and rasped off sharp corners. The Foredom and rotary rasp again did some shaping, while the Dumore die grinder hogged off wood in a fury of slow-to-settle dust. And the Foredom with its double-cut bit again did its job of taking

away coarse marks left by the other tools. But much of the final shaping, especially of the bill, was yet to be done—but with a knife, not motor-driven tools.

I had heard it said by carvers such as Larry Hayden that areas like the eyes and bill, when not well done, will disqualify many otherwise fine carvings in competitions. Yet, with the advent of the study bill, accuracy has taken the place of guesswork. But it is a part of the duck's anatomy that may have more subtleties and changes in shape than any other.

The Mandibles

A duck's bill consists of an upper and lower mandible, the upper one having nostrils that actually pass through the bill to form a kind of corridor, and what is

Then the top view of the gadwall head is bandsawed to shape.

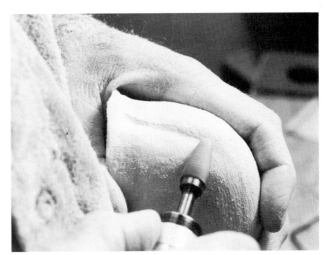

This double-cut carbide bit is used to shape the head and make a depression for the nape.

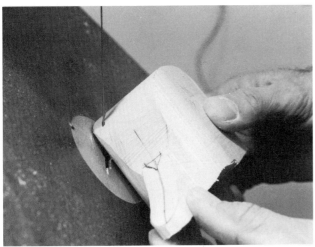

As he did with the body, Jim uses a skip-tooth blade to rasp off the sharp corners of the wood, which makes grinding in the next steps easier.

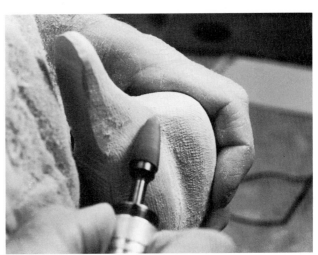

The same bit defines the eye sockets.

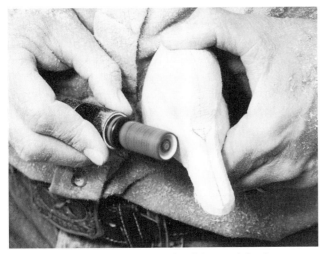

The Foredom, a Pfingst & Company handpiece, and the three-quarter-inch-diameter rasp used in previous steps are used to refine some areas around the bill.

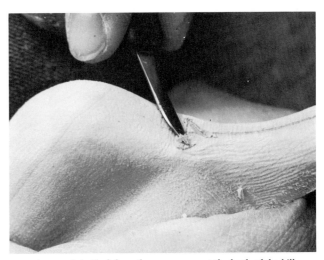

A carver's knife defines the ogee curves at the back of the bill.

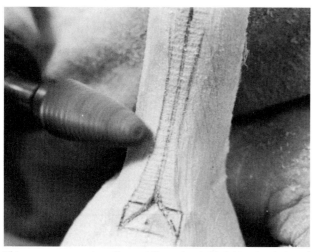

This concave area where the nostrils are located is laid out and shaped with the double-cut bit.

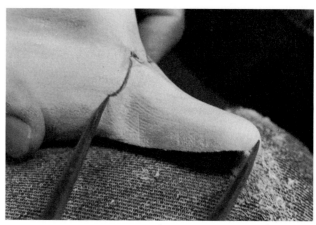

Here Jim brings the measurement to the wood. Note the extra wood he has left beneath the bill. Jim feels this is insurance against the bill starting out too thin.

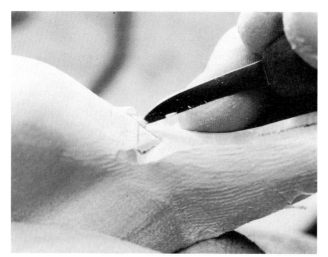

Here Jim lowers the back portion of the bill into the head to create a tiny shelf.

A critical measurement to be transferred from the study bill to the wood is the length of the upper mandible or jaw.

called a nail (a kind of nub) on the very end. There are also wrinkles, and at times even the tiny serrations called lamellae can be seen.

But Jim first went at the ogee curve with the knife, shaping it with the point (knifemakers are listed in the Appendix). When satisfied, he then took two more critical measurements from the study bill: one from the point where the mandibles hinge to the outermost tip of the nail, the other from the same hinge to the top of one side of the ogee. With these transferred to the wood, Jim began to draw on lines that represent where the two mandibles meet. These he would define with a straight down or stop cut, using the point of the knife.

Jim uses knives made specifically for the carver by Cheston Knotts and Robert Lominack. Both kinds are super, he said, with both needing only occasional sharpening on a leather strop with rouge powder. But he would seem to favor an X-acto knife over the others. He likes the wooden-handled type, with an interchangeable blade mechanism. Preferring a No. 11 blade, he can discard it for another when it gets dull or broken. He will use this same X-acto knife later when defining feathers.

While working, Jim told me he finds it interesting to compare study bills of the same species, and to use both for critical measurements. He showed me two for a gadwall drake, one dark and solid looking, the other light, cream-colored, and fragile in appearance. But the details on the second were exceptional, down to the very teeth. Yet, they were different in another way. Jim said one was smaller, cast perhaps from a younger bird.

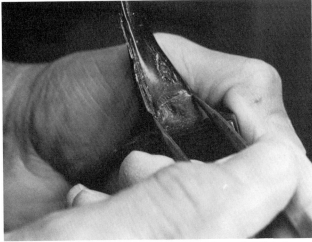

The second critical measurement taken from the study bill is from a point at the rear of the mandibles to the top of an ogee curve.

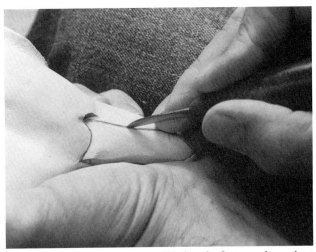

To begin to achieve the upper mandible line, he first cuts down about one-sixteenth inch with a knife. This is one kind of stop cut.

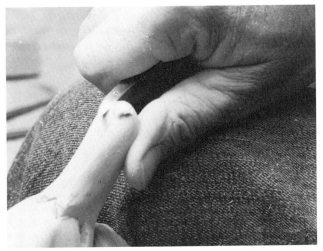

Before Jim starts defining the mandibles, he first shapes the tip of the bill, or nail, with fine knife work.

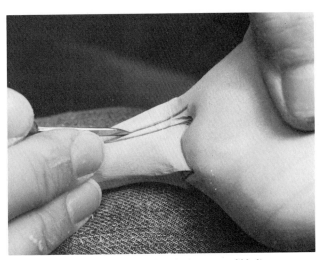

Another stop cut establishes the lower mandible line.

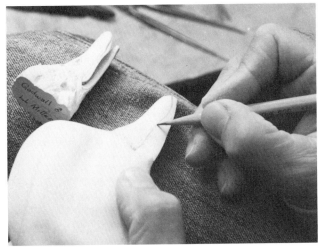

Jim may use more than one study bill as a reference when establishing the anatomy. Here he determines the division between the mandibles.

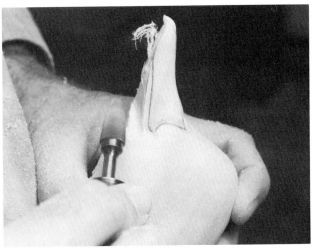

Once these mandible lines are established, he can grind away the extra wood beneath the bill with his double-cut cutter.

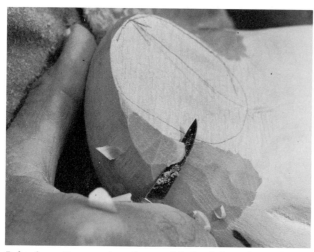

Before he continues work on the rest of the head, Jim reshapes the area where the head and breast meet.

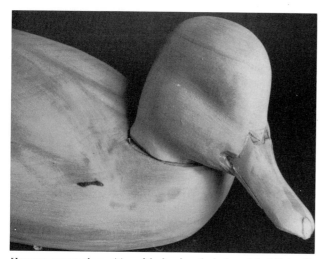

Here you can see the position of the head on the body and the bill details.

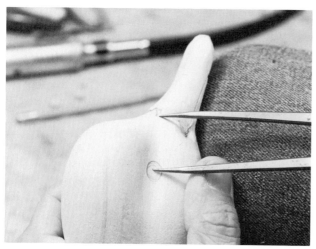

Laying out the eyes is next. The measurement he is making is one taken from a live bird and is used for all his gadwall carvings. It is from the upper point of an ogee curve to the center of an eye socket. It is imperative, then, to completely shape the bill before locating the eyes.

Drawing the knife along the scribed lines and without stopping, Jim said, "When a knife follows a pencil line in defining the bill mandibles, it's important that the knife is perpendicular to the wood. If you move it over to one side or the other, it's going to distort the details. It's almost the same with the burning pen. Lay that over left or right, ten or fifteen degrees, and you're burning a wider line, which is not really what you want. It's the same with the knife."

Lifelike Eyes

The next step was to lay out the eye positions, deep holes to be filled with glass. Jim was not without comments as he began determining where those eyes should be with his calipers. "One of the hardest things for me to overcome was getting the head and eyes to look accurate and lifelike. If you're looking at a carving, you're basically looking into its eyes. Looking at another person, you're looking at the eyes, the mouth, the face. What I'm trying to say is, I'm trying to make the head, the eyes, and the bill look good."

From his references, he took a dusty piece of paper, with two pencil points on it. Written underneath was "Eye Measurement." It was another standard measurement, one he had taken from a freshly killed duck, that gave him the distance from the top of one side of the ogee to the center of the eye socket.

He continued to talk as one point of the calipers left a small hole on either side of the head. "The rest of the carving has to be good, but more time should be spent in the area you're going to be looking at. It's a good rule of thumb: Let the head be the focal point."

After he had driven an icepick into the center of the sockets, leaving a deep mark, he went back to the Foredom and chucked up a round, ball-shaped bit. This ground away wood where he had located the eyes. Above the noise of the grinding, Jim said, "From the eye socket to the base of the bill, there's a channel. It almost stands to reason that a bird couldn't see out over this area unless there were this channel."

Floating the Eyes

Jim suspended the head between icepick and pencil, the bill projected toward his face. "I do not predrill my eye sockets from the pattern itself. If ever there was any type of change in the measurement or length of the bill, which easily happens when carving, and the eyehole is already drilled, there's no latitude for

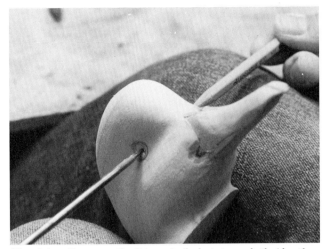

Though he will measure the distance in the last step on both sides, these two sharp objects will insure the symmetry of the eyes.

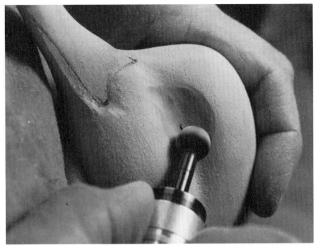

A small dental bit and a Dremel Moto Tool have deepened the holes left by an ice pick. A round cutter can then deepen the eye socket without totally removing the marks for the socket centers.

change. I'd rather carve the head, have that accurate, and work backward to the eye socket. When I locate one, I then line up this pick and pencil visually to locate the other."

The Foredom was not off for long. A twist of the chuck and a new bit was inserted into the handpiece. Jim described it as a cone-shaped reamer. Holding the head securely in one hand, he drove the point of the bit into the holes left by the icepick. When finished, the head had a strange look, more skull-like than ducklike.

Jim explained his boring technique. "I put the eye socket in so that it is canted toward the tip of the bill. That is, I put the cone in at an angle. I also make the hole large enough so that the eyes float in there."

What does he mean by floating? "That's only a temporary term. Since the first eye is easy to mount, it's the second one that has to be matched with the existing eye. So by having the hole just a little on the large side, filled with my plumber's seal, I have some latitude with the other eye. That's why it will float until the seal hardens the eye in place."

Plumber's seal or sealant, a two-part epoxy, is not the only material that Jim sets eyes in. He has discovered, probably after trying a variety of materials never meant to be applied to the faces of wooden ducks, a wood filler labeled 3-in-1 Plastic Wood to do the job. It is what he applies around the eyes to give that tight look of feathered flesh and eyeball.

He applied the wood fill quickly, working it around the glass with a small carver's chisel, smoothing out what he could. But what he calls "feathering," the real smoothing or finishing, is done with the 3-in-1 solvent

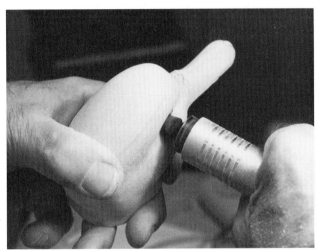

A sharply pointed reamer bit makes the actual holes for the eyes. Note that he cants the handpiece and bit slightly forward. This will help achieve the expression he wants with the glass eyes he will put in later.

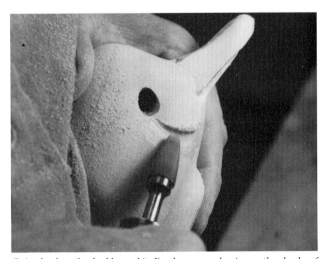

Going back to the double-cut bit, Jim does some shaping on the cheeks of the gadwall.

and a sable brush, another technique he happened onto. "As long as the Plastic Wood is kept solvent, you can work it almost indefinitely. And feathering with a brush means very little sanding in the end."

He said he sets the eyes into plumber's seal and not Plastic Wood because the former does not dry as quickly as the latter, which gives him more time to "float the eyes around" and get the right symmetry. "But keep that plumber's seal off your fingers," he warned. "If you do touch the bird with it, you'll leave traces of it. And that's where the paint won't stick later on. And you won't be able to burn quill and barb lines later on. That's why I use Plastic Wood on the outside of the eye. It does burn, contrary to what people might tell you."

Jim shared with me his annoyance with people who discredit wood filler such as this product. "I heard all along that you can't burn Plastic Wood, that it will pull away from the body. But perhaps it's my nature that, before I believe anything, I have to try it. I'm glad I did. It can be burned, but part of that is due to these new rheostat burners that allow me to burn at a low temperature. I just don't know how you could get the realism around the eye if you didn't use Plastic Wood. I can't burn an epoxy sealer or Tuf-carv or Tuf-fil, but I sure can this."

He firmly believes that setting the eyes is something extra time should be devoted to. "It's so important that the eye sockets are perfect. Make sure one eye socket is not higher than the other and that you can see the same amount of wood from the back part of them from both sides. Also, I want to be able to look straight down from above the head and not be able to see the glass eyes."

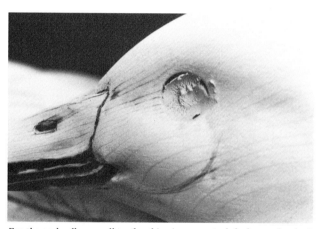

For the gadwall, as well as for this cinnamon teal drake, a plumber's two-part epoxy sealer is used to fill in the eye sockets. In this, which hardens slowly, the eyes can be "floated" or positioned for the right look.

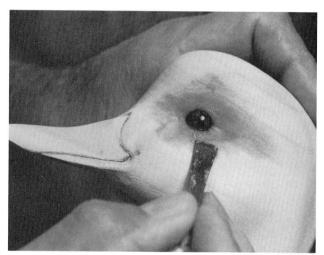

3-in-1 makes a solvent that Jim uses to work the wood filler. It will keep the filler soft and pliable, and can be worked first with a chisel and finally with a sable brush.

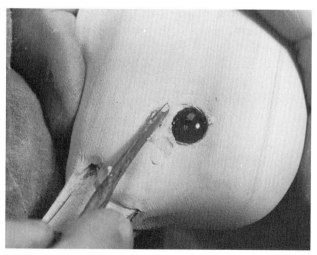

Back to the gadwall, with the epoxy having hardened overnight, the eyes are enclosed with 3-in-1 Plastic Wood, worked here with a small gouge.

Here the cinnamon teal drake has had each eye enclosed with the Plastic Wood. Jim calls the working of it "feathering."

Jim held the back of the head in front of me. "Look straight down," he said. "At this point, you'll see just a fraction of brown on both sides. If I saw a lot on one side and none on the other, I'd be in big trouble. I have to see the same amount of wood carved away or left on both sides before I apply the Plastic Wood around the eyes. Seeing this depends on how accurately I drilled in the eye sockets and how accurately I carved the cheeks. So much of this has been learned by trial and error."

It was not coincidental that Jim told me, around nine on our first evening together, that "I like to set my eyes as the last thing for the day so that the next morning they'll be well hardened." We had finished a great deal during one day.

Back to the Bill

Much more refining went into the bill that next morning, both on the upper and lower mandibles. Most of it was knife work, some with a small ruby carver and Foredom. Of the ruby carvers (the supplier is listed in the Appendix), he said, "The best advantage of these bits is that you don't have to do much sanding when you're finished with them. I guess their basic asset is that they cut wood away without tearing it. Other cutters have that tendency. And they don't clog with wood."

But these were not the only tools used. Jim also applied the burning tool and its pen to enscribe bill wrinkles and mandible serrations, creases under the bill, and the stop cuts made by the carver's knife.

The burning pen will refine the stop cuts without

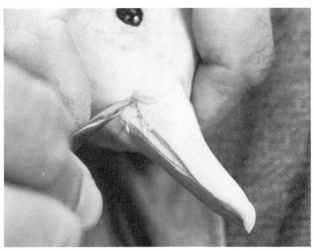

Next he relieves wood in the corner of the upper and lower mandibles with a knife so that the lower mandible can fit into the upper.

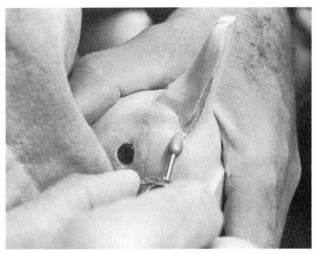

A ruby carver (see Appendix for address of supplier, Elkay Products) takes wood away from behind that same corner of the mandibles. This gives the illusion of a duck's "smile."

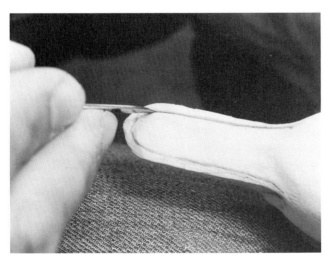

Back to the bill, Jim starts to carve the underpart of the lower mandible.

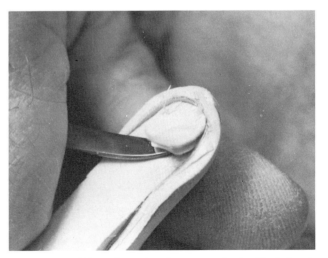

The lower mandible angles up into the upper at the tip. Wood there is removed.

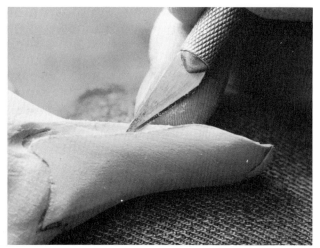

An X-acto knife and its interchangeable No. 11 blade separate the upper and lower mandibles where they come together.

making them bigger. But it can also polish or smooth out the facets left by even the best knife work, a "burnishing with heat" technique.

Where had this technique come from? Jim answered: "When I started carving, I had better control over a burning pen than I did with a knife. So I do a lot of work on the bill with it. I guess you could also call it carving or shaping with heat. But whichever, it takes the hard edges off knife cuts." He added that sandpaper could then be used to remove the charred wood residue left by the burning.

But Jim pondered some more and mentioned George Walker's name. "He was quick to point out new things in carving. I think it might have been

The inner edge of the upper mandible must now be refined with a knife.

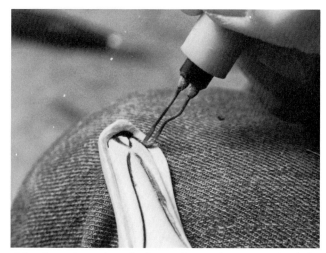

A burning tool (see Appendix for suppliers) and pen are used to refine and shape with heat the elongated V and the mandible separation.

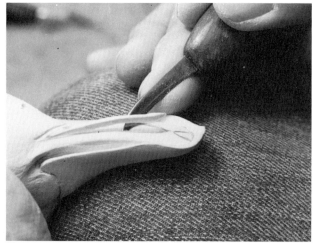

The underside of a duck's bill has a long V-like area that is lower than the rest of the bill, but it is also slightly convex in shape. This is defined with a knife.

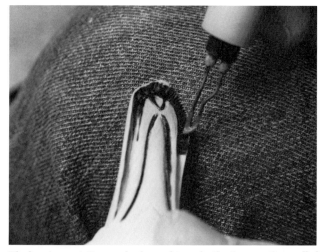

The burning pen's tip can also be used to make the tiny serrations called lamellae on the underside of the bill.

George who triggered the thought process that got me to use this burning tool to do shaping."

Mandible Angles and Unexpected Repairs.

Jim pointed out, as he refined the underside of the bill, that the lower mandible comes up into the upper one slightly. "The angle that it comes off the jaw is very important. I've seen carvings where, if the lower mandible were extended by an imaginary line, it would come up through the middle of the bill. This is not correct."

Taking some time to look out at the aviary birds, watching a regal-looking baikal teal take to the water

With the burning pen, he can actually carve wood away.

In addition, the pen can create what Jim describes as a withered effect on the underside.

Jim strengthens the nail on the upper mandible with Wonder Bond, a cyanoacrylate.

The upper mandible has a rolled lip edge. This Jim begins to define with the carver's knife.

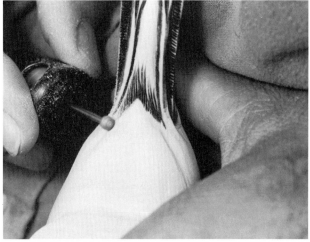

For further refinement, a one-eighth-inch diameter ruby carver creates a depression underneath the head.

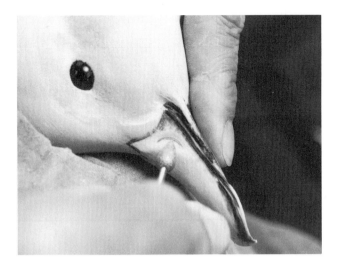

with a pace faster than its pen mates, I heard a stern "damn" come from Jim. He had been working the knife around the front of the bill that forms what is anatomically called a nail. The tip had loosened, nearly coming off the bill.

Jim did not seem too disheartened and took from a shelf a small, squarish, white tube. It was Wonder Bond, a clear glue that could repair damaged bills and feather tips. But he said he would not use it for gluing pieces back on, but only for reinforcing weakened ones.

Pierced Nostrils

A few carvers make use of the Dremel Moto Tool, a grinder with its motor in its handpiece. When interviewing Gary Yoder and Larry Barth for *How to Carve Wildfowl*, I had seen them use it. But Jim's only use for it is to pierce his ducks' nostrils. This he can do with a small dental bit, working his way in from both sides until light appears through the nasal channel. "Use the Dremel for more than that, like trying to hog wood off, and you'll burn out its motor," Jim said.

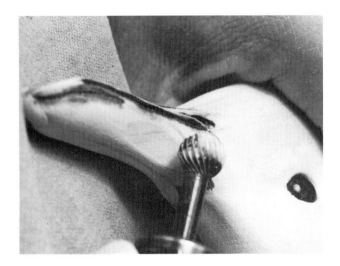

Behind the Bill

Jim had not finished with the Plastic Wood. As he brought out the can, he admitted that he has trouble redefining the area directly above the bill of a duck. It is a difficult transition area, he explained, one where hard and soft lines merge, and convexing and flat

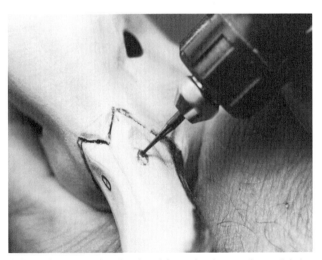

A Dremel Moto Tool and a dental bit make the actual nostril holes, which form a continuous channel through the bill.

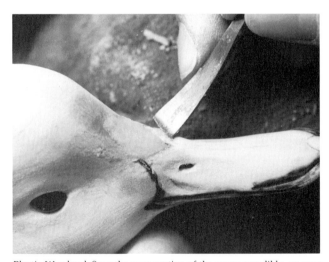

Plastic Wood redefines the ogee portion of the upper mandible, an area Jim finds difficult to shape with a knife or grinding bits due to its difficult curves. This, like the eye sockets, is feathered with 3-in-1 solvent, chisel, and brush.

Head feathers and their flow are laid out with a pencil.

areas blend. "The knife seems to chew up the area instead of carving it. So I'll redefine and redress the area by feathering in the Plastic Wood."

Flow Lines

The eyes were in place, the bill well detailed. And the head had yet to be joined to the body. But before attaching it, Jim had still more operations to perform on the gadwall head: stoning and burning.

I first thought that feathers are simply drawn on the head, moving them from the bill to the crown and back, with enough variety to avoid what has been described by carvers as the fishscale look. But Jim is too well versed in duck details. Instead, he begins drawing lines, "flow lines" he calls them, from the corners of the bill and eyes. These indicate the flow of the feathers.

Jim is categorical about the line details. "You can't do too much pencil work as you're going along." But references are always kept in view. "When drawing feathers on the bird, even the head, I'm either looking at study mounts or pictures. Plus, I've taken a lot of photos looking down on birds either from above an aviary, from my window here, or of a bird held in someone else's hands."

As the lines engulfed the head, he said, perhaps as an afterthought, "You never know a subject so well

Feathers are relieved with a cylinder-shaped sanding attachment, handpiece, and Foredom. Jim works from the base of the neck forward so he does not sand away the next feather outline.

that you give up on a reference. Sometimes I think I can do this with my eyes closed, but I need reassurance, so I go back to the reference."

Penciled feathers followed quickly, and these were relieved with a small sanding attachment and Foredom. Jim explained that he works from the back forward so that the drum does not grind away the pencil lines. But instead of using the burning pen to put in feather details, Jim brought out a long, thin grinding stone, also Foredom adaptable. With the edge of the

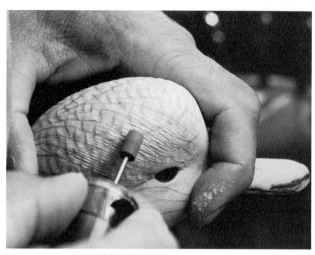

A stoning attachment follows the flow lines. These give the feathers more depth.

Here the gadwall head can be seen completely stoned.

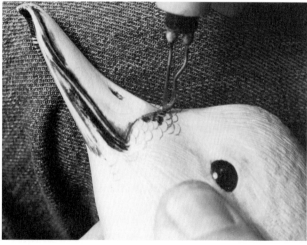

Jim will next burn over the stoning grooves, adding yet another depth or dimension of realism to the bird. But around the bill, he burns in individual feathers that cannot be done with a sanding drum.

stone, he filled in the areas between and in the direction of the flow lines with hundreds of grooves.

Jim produced a worn and dusty clump of steel wool from a corner of his workbench. "There is always an area of basswood where you can see, when going against the grain, a fuzziness. Steel wool or even a stiff bristle brush will help remove it. Even a metal suede brush will do the trick. But always," Jim said, as he rubbed the duck with hard stokes, "go with the grain, or you'll create more fuzziness.

"I use 000 steel wool. This will feather the little edges off, so when I'm burning, I'll end up with a softer surface." When finished, he then heated his burning pen and burned over the shallow grooves left by the stoning.

Why both stone and burn? I asked him about this technique, which he would later use for the entire body of the gadwall. And why do so much work on the head before it was attached to the body? The answer to my first question involves the depth, Jim said. "Stoning gives the bird a coarse look. But more important, when under the burning lines, it gives added depth which will come through even when the bird is painted." In answer to the second question, he told me he could put in better detail more easily with the head in his hands. "I'll do the head totally before I affix it to the body because the head, with all its little feathers, is much easier to handle when it's off the body."

"But I don't put details on the head, do the burning and stoning that is, until the eyes are in. Obviously you noticed that. I do it that way so I don't have to go over the Plastic Wood a second time with the stone and burning pen. Also, the set-in eyes give me a truer picture of the bird."

On with the Head

Burned and stoned, the head was ready to give the basswood body its real identity. The process of joining head to body was not much different from the techniques used for setting in the eyes. But instead of plumber's seal, it was a Devcon two-part epoxy that bonded the two pieces of wood together in just minutes. And it was the Plastic Wood, feathered with solvent and sable brush, that disguised the glue joint.

Working quickly so that the Plastic Wood did not dry out on him, Jim said, "I try not to put on too much at a time. I try to put on half and feather that with the solvent. The first couple of times you do this, you may not be totally pleased. But you can always take some

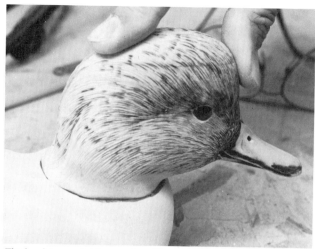

The head is completely stoned and burned before being attached to the body. For this, he uses Devcon five-minute epoxy and maintains slight pressure.

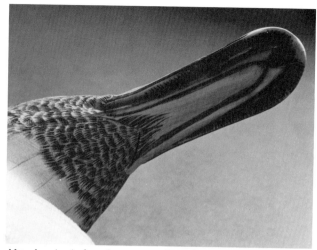

More burning is done, however, on the underside of the cinnamon teal head.

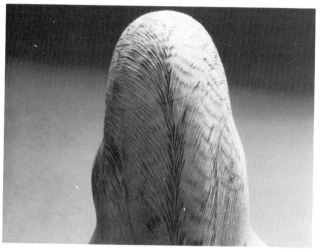

Not all of the back of the head of the gadwall is burned. Note how the relieved feathers show through the stoning grooves.

The head and body seam is covered with Plastic Wood, and worked and feathered as were the eyes and ogee area of the bill.

Here is an opportunity to view the finished underportion of the bill and the lines of stoning and burning. Jim says it is much easier to do these operations on the head when it is separate from the body.

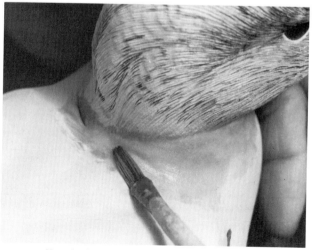

Here the filler is feathered with solvent and a brush.

This photo shows the materials and the bird with finished neck.

Plastic Wood and put on a skim coat or carve some away if you get too much on the neck."

More Identity

There was one more step to be taken with the head, and that was to build up, with a previously used material, three small areas: the eyelids, the nostrils, and the base of the lower mandible.

Jim brought out the same two-part plumber's seal he had used when setting the eyes into the head. Now he would use it externally on the bird. "I use Atlas Plumber's Seal, and probably a plumbing supply store is where you can purchase it. I take a thin strip of it that I roll out on my Sanolite chopping block, and then

The head of this canvasback drake is joined to the body. Note the bill details, the stoning and burning on the head.

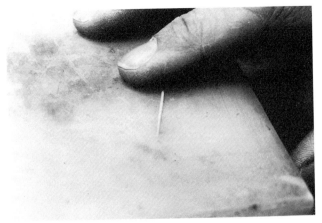

Finishing touches on the gadwall and other ducks are made around the eyes, the nostrils, and the corners of the mouth. These are done with the same material used to hold the eyes in place, the plumber's epoxy sealer. Here it is rolled into thin strips on a plastic chopping block.

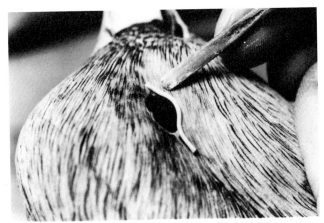

The first place it is applied is around the eyes, acting as lids. Jim uses a small gouge to apply the material.

work it with a brush around the eyes, the nostrils and the lower mandible. It takes eight to ten hours to set up, so it's another of those jobs to leave for the last of the evening. Notice I take a wetted brush and move the thin pieces around with it." Jim gave a muted laugh. "You may want to scream the first time you try it, but ultimately it is well worth the trouble. But remember, it's easier to work when it's soft and pliable. So if it starts to harden up, throw it out and work with a fresh piece."

He advises that you "roll out the plumber's seal with the heel of the hand. It adheres better if the area it's to be applied to is dampened. That way, it will stick and not move around." Jim keeps a can of water at hand to dip the sable brush into.

The timing had been good. It was evening, after eight, and much more had been done during the first two days than I had anticipated. But I had another

question to ask Jim before we finished for the evening. It had been asked of me by the editor of a new magazine, *Wildfowl Carving and Collecting*. She wanted to know how Jim got "the look" she believed his ducks have.

He paused, looking up and out the darkened window toward the house with its lit panes white against the night. "Well, part of it is positioning the eyes. But I'm not sure you can tell someone how to capture realism, if that's what she means. I can tell people how I do it, but that doesn't guarantee that character or realism will be achieved."

He said there are really only two distinct looks that can be created. "One is to make the eyes wide open,

A closeup of the bill shows the dramatic effect the material has on the nostril. And though barely perceptible, it emphasizes the bird's "smile."

This hardener and resin combination is slow to set up and is water soluble, allowing it to be worked into place with water and a sable brush.

The final place for the epoxy sealer is around the nostril holes. Here Jim feathers it out with a brush and water.

Shown here are the three areas the sealer was applied to.

For an interesting contrast, compare the head of the cinnamon teal before the plumber's sealer is applied. Also study the burning lines on this duck.

The canvasback in the rear is burned, but without its lids, built-up nostrils, and smile. The foreground duck is completed.

almost bug-eyed. But when I'm applying the plumber's seal, I like to have the lids drawn in at the corners just a bit. It makes the bird look more intelligent, more curious. Maybe it's more pleasing to the observer to have something more relaxed than bugged wide open."

The other distinctive look, Jim said, is a mean one. "If you want to do that, you build up over the eyes with a little extra plastic wood. It gives the bird a scowl. I do that on my shovelers. There are little muscles over their eyes, and when I make them, people will tell me the ducks look mean."

He admitted that at one time, the eyes were a weak area for him. "It used to drive me crazy trying to get my birds more lifelike. I guess a lot has to do with how I build up the Plastic Wood and the plumber's seal around the eyes. I just don't try to open up the eye so that it is perfectly round. That's only for when a bird is startled. I think when they're relaxed, there's a cup to the lids. But whether I'm right or wrong, I get a lot of favorable comments on this."

Body Feathers

Much of the following day's work involved laying out feathers on the body, drawing and redrawing

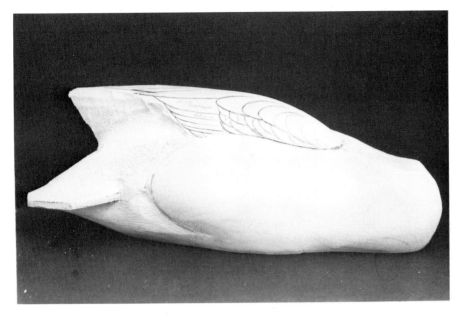

Here can be seen the cinnamon teal's side pocket and tail area, defined with the speculum, scapulars, and some of the tertials drawn on the wood.

The carver's knife outlines the tertials going one-sixteenth-inch deep. Also note the feather splits or separations along an edge.

The template for these tertial feathers was taken from a study skin. Note that Jim lays out one side at a time because the underlying primary groupings will come off higher on one side. The side opposite of that he is working on will have to be reduced slightly in thickness.

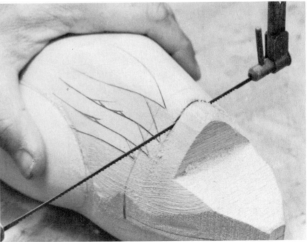

Since more wood was left during the original bandsawing than was needed, a coping saw helps remove it.

them, referring to a study mount of a gadwall. But even with the mount present, Jim was not casual with the layout. Here too he sketched the flow lines for the feathers on the sides, making his curving lines, that would help when it came to stoning in the texture of the feathers.

As he sketched around his tertial feather templates taken from his gadwall envelope, he said, "I think you have to be prepared to draw and redraw feathers. So have a good, sharp No. 2 pencil handy, and don't be afraid to erase and start over. It's a lot easier to take your time when doing this. Think it through and don't

Wood is cut away between the tertial tips with a knife.

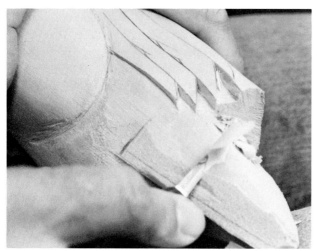

Wood is then pared away on the tail area.

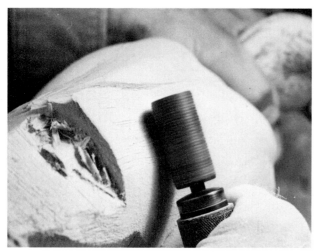

Jim can now lower the left-hand side (as seen head on) of the tertial area to enable the primaries, which will be inserted after the bird is completely painted, to cross.

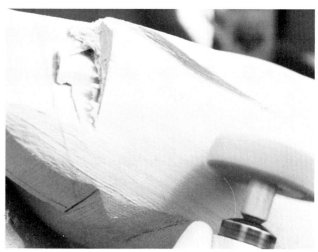

That same side is smoothed before the tertials are laid out in pencil.

rush. Eventually you're going to have to relief some feathers and you don't want to worry that it's coming off in the wrong places. The bottom line is to be methodical and get it done right."

And shortcuts, he noted, are catastrophic. "Anything that's done quickly is usually reflected in the end product."

Perhaps as an aside, Jim said, "It really helps to be able to draw feathers on the bird. I think it's difficult for a lot of people. I know it didn't come easily to me. But it does come with practice and studying birds."

He pointed out that the tertials he was outlining would be reliefed about a half-inch from the rest of the body, and that these and other back feathers would be outlined with a knife and burning pen, a technique he used on the bill. He had some specific advice on tertials, slowly putting his words together. "What I try to do when laying out the tertials on the gadwall is to make an irregular pattern. I get hung up on the fact that there's little symmetry on a duck. Occasionally I'll see a bird in the aviary that has some continuity on both sides, but rarely do you see perfect layout. I guess I use some imagination here when everything is not balanced."

But Jim had a warning to give concerning mounted birds. He has found that their feathers may actually be worn down in size and, therefore, do not give a true measurement. I assumed his mount was a good one, for he took a small flexible ruler often to the back of the bird. Yet, he said, even if a mount's feathers were in perfect condition, the feather sizes might vary as much as an inch. Did that mean one gadwall was

Now Jim lays out the four tertials on the right side.

The cylindrical rasp, which was used to shape and refine in previous steps, now separates the tail from the rump.

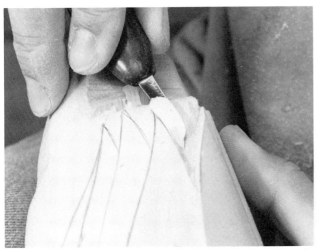

More wood is worked away from between the tertials. Note how the right top tertial is slightly higher than the adjacent one.

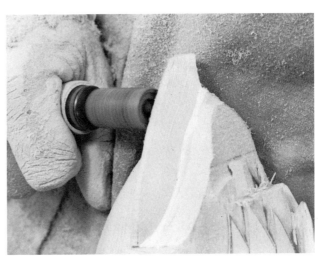

The same attachment relieves wood from underneath the tail. Jim notes that the rump extends to the end of the tail on the gadwall.

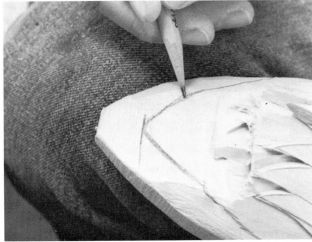

The tail area, which is obviously thinner than the body, is drawn on the wood.

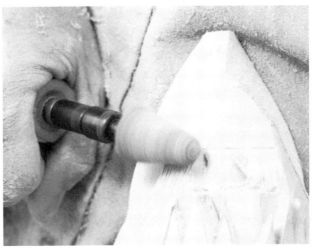

The cone-shaped carbide burr and Dumore die grinder slope the upper rump area, removing wood quickly.

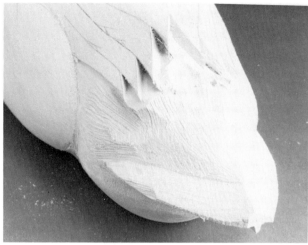

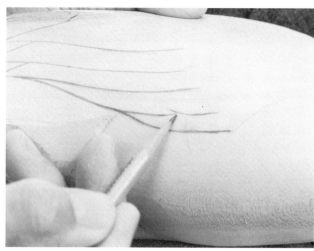

This photo shows the correct anatomical shape of the tail and rump. Note also the relieved tertials.

Jim points out that he has put in a feather split to bring a bit of the white of the speculum up under the adjoining gray feathers.

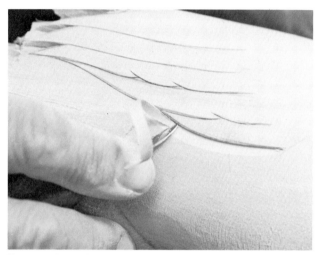

Here Jim relieves the speculum slightly. This is the area on the secondary wing feathers that is usually brightly colored. On the gadwall drake it is white.

Jim proceeds to lay out the scapulars, those feathers on the shoulders just above the wings. Note that he uses a good mount to determine the positions of these feathers.

Here is the layout of all scapulars and small back feathers.

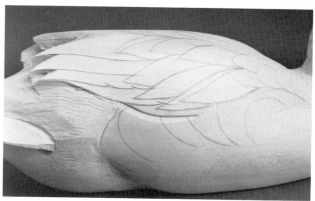

On the cinnamon teal drake, most of the feathers on the back have been laid out.

Back to the gadwall, you can see the scapulars and what will be feather groupings on the side pockets.

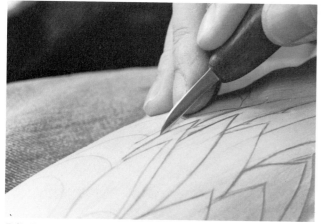

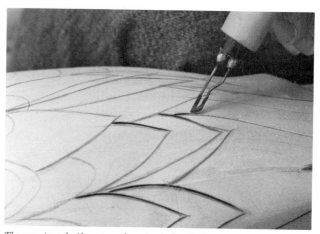

Relieving the back feathers begins not with a chisel but with a knife. This is really a channel for the next step.

The previous knife cut made a track for the burning pen, which, Jim says, gives a wider line or slot to chisel away wood from around the feathers.

The results of outlining with the burning pen can be seen on the cinnamon teal.

This photo can be studied for the anatomy of the rump and tail.

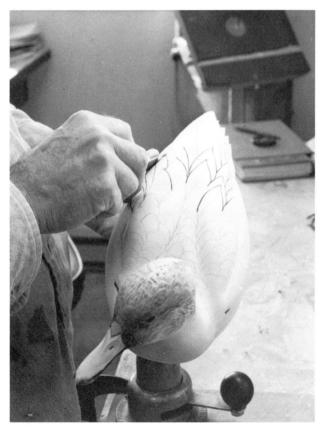

For the best control of the chisel that will relieve the back feathers, Jim must have both hands free. He mounts the gadwall, then, on a Wilton power vise which allows the work to be rotated and pivoted.

more adult than another? That was not necessarily so, he answered.

Jim added that the feathers themselves may be different – some squarish, some round. "So it's important to study the feathers of the particular bird you're working on to pick up these things. But be careful, whatever your feather design, that you don't make them look like scales. Some people get so carried away making feathers on the back and rump areas that they make the duck look like a pine cone. Now ocasionally if one comes up out of the water, you might get a look like that when it shakes itself. But it's not a pleasing way to do them, nor is it a way people see waterfowl."

Feathers Like Tents

Before I left for home, Jim outlined the feathers he had drawn on the gadwall's flanks with a ball-shaped cutter. Of that cutter, he said, "It cuts sharp enough so you don't have to do much sanding. There are some bits you use for reliefing that chew up the wood. Even the ruby carver doesn't do quite as good a job as this cutter."

Between grindings, he told me that he sees feathers shaped almost like tents. "That is, I don't see them as being perfectly flat. Consequently, I try to carve them

A one-quarter-inch chisel relieves the feathers previously outlined with the knife and burning pen.

Jim says it is important to make feathers "tented," that is, high where the quills are and tapered down from them. Here you can see how he works at that shaping strategy.

with a tentlike appearance, meaning the quill is at the high point." It was obvious to me that the large channels the cutter left around the feathers also left a high spot made possible by the natural curvature of the duck's body.

He had also started reliefing the tertials. But this was an operation that required two hands free to work the tools, not only defining the tertial ends but also relieving or removing wood from their undersides, thus allowing them to project naturally away from the body.

To free his hands, Jim uses a power vise. Able to lock in different positions, it secures the bird from underneath with a detachable bracket. With the gadwall held this way well above the surface of the workbench, Jim shaved away wood with a small chisel, similar to or perhaps the same that had applied Plastic Wood to the neck and eyes. The wood was removed quickly but carefully so that the feather tips did not become too fragile. While working, he said to me, "I'm not sure tupelo gum holds up as well when undercutting areas like the tertials. But I've been watching other carvers use it to see the results."

He went on to say that at one time in his carving career he would insert these tertials, as he would later do with the gadwall's primaries. He admitted that he even made the tail feathers as separate pieces. "But somewhere over the years, I decided they looked better the way I do them now, no matter how well I may have done inserts."

Jim reflected a moment and said, "Yes, they look better if you can get them all in one piece. You see, the

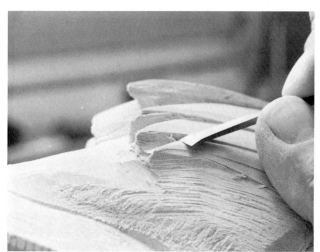

Jim chisels away at the tertials, making sure they are not flat.

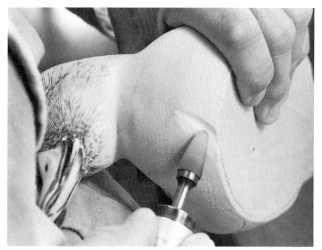

Jim points out that there can be a sizable split on the breast of a duck. Grinding this into the wood adds an interesting feature to the bird.

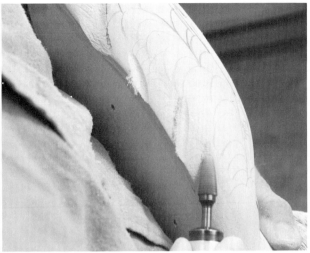

Jim puts in grooves on the lower sides to accommodate feather patterns to be made later.

Back to the steel ball cutter, Jim relieves slightly the side pocket feathers, again with the intention of giving them a puffy look.

A one-half-inch diameter steel cutter relieves feathers on the back. This bit gives them a puffy look.

Here are the finished results after grinding and sanding by hand.

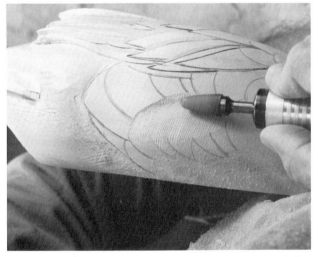

To separate two groups of feathers on a side pocket, Jim forms a shallow valley with his cone-shaped double-cut bit.

biggest problem is that you get a flat surface when you make an insert. Then it's hard to get the feathers tented or high at the quill."

A Faint Rattle

When I returned two weeks later, Jim had stoned both sides of the gadwall and burned one side. I held the bird in my hand, appreciating the textures he had given the bird, looking for the depth he told me that stoning and burning, one underneath the other, would achieve. The bird was taking on a crafted character as his tools defined and refined the anatomy.

But something rattled faintly from within the bird. I thought a piece of lead balancing weight had come

The effects of this low-relief work can be seen on the back of the finished gadwall, even through the paint.

loose. I asked Jim about it. He laughed softly and told me it was a nail inside the gadwall. He explained that much of his tertial and tail feathers were reliefed with the bird mounted on the power vise, which requires the bottom of the duck to be secured to a plate. The screws will penetrate the plug slightly, leaving minute openings that can be sealed before the bird is floated again. Through one of them Jim inserts a nail, a wire brad really. "I do this so people will know that the bird is hollow. Picking up a hollow bird gives me a nice feel as opposed to one that is solid."

Splitting for Color

Jim said that feather barbs are not just a series of somewhat parallel lines. They may also bunch together to form splits, many occurring naturally at the waterline when the feathers get wet. "That's something you pick up from photographs. You don't have nearly as many splits when the feathers are dry." But Jim will also put in splits, whether by using the point of the knife or burning away wood, in areas where they would not normally be found. This he calls "artistic license," explaining, "On this gadwall, there's going to be a bit of rust color of the upper coverts exposed on one side. There I can make little feather splits. They enhance the carving where other colors are added. They seem to bring your eye to that area and give the bird some more realism." He also pointed out an area on a mount he described as the speculum, a white patch, which clearly showed through other feathers. It was on the left side, toward the rear and

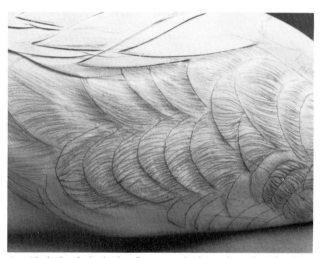

As with the head, the feather flow must also be made on the sides. Here flow lines are penciled on the wood. Note that the lines go in slightly different directions.

Splits are then made with a knife.

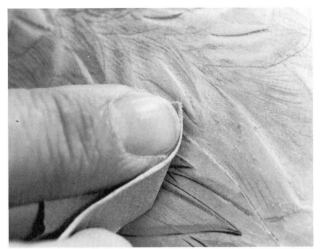

The edges of the splits are softened with 220-grit sandpaper.

On the finished gadwall, the effects of relieving the side pocket feathers, the splitting, and the stoning can be seen.

The results of splitting can be seen here. Jim says that at water level, more splits will be present, something he has learned from all his reference material.

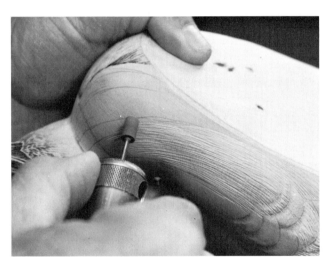

With the same attachment, Jim stones from under the chin into the side pockets.

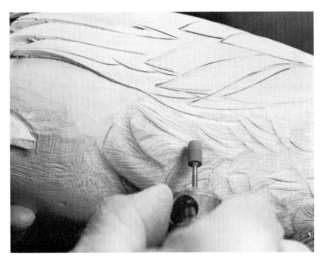

The next step is stoning. Being used is a one-quarter-inch-diameter by three-eights-inch-long cylindrical stone.

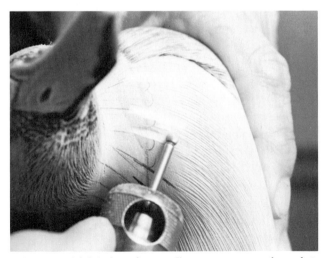

Using a one-eighth-inch steel cutter, Jim puts grooves on the neck to define small feather groupings that run vertically.

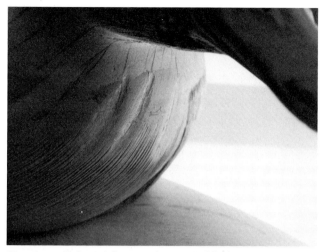

Here the small channels between those vertical feather groupings can be seen.

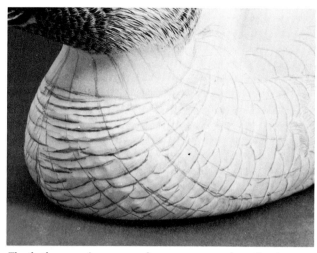

The feather groupings are much more pronounced on the cinnamon teal's breast than on the gadwall's. These too have been relieved.

The cinnamon teal has progressed to nearly the same stage as the gadwall drake. The side pocket feathers have their flow lines, but they have yet to be stoned.

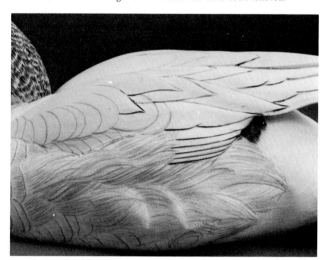

The layout of the flow lines on the cinnamon teal's right side can be studied here. In the center of the photo is the speculum, which has been outlined with the knife and burning pen.

The opposite side pocket of the cinnamon teal has been stoned.

This photo shows the layout of the scapulars and breast feathers.

And this photo shows where the leg of what will be a face-scratching duck is to be located.

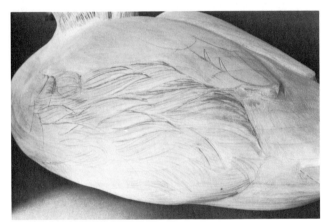

A closer view of the canvasback gives side pocket feather layout and flow lines.

Jim has relieved the side pocket feathers of the canvasback drake. Notice how pointed they are in contrast to the gadwall's and cinnamon teal's.

One final view of the canvasback shows the dramatic feather groupings on the left side pocket. Note also the bill detail.

One final view of the cinnamon teal shows the stoning of the breast feathers and the details of the bill. Note the depressions along the upper mandible and the deeper nostril depressions. Also note the fairly coarse head feathers in contrast to the gadwall's and how the eyes look slightly forward.

directly above the gadwall's webbed foot. It would be in approximately the same place on the wooden gadwall, Jim said.

A Cordless Burning Pen?

Jim did a great deal of burning that day, many hours worth while I photographed carved birds in his personal collection. He said that he preferred The Detailer burning pen (see Appendix for supplier) because of the different tips that can be purchased. "I like the really sharp points," he said. "You get a feel for what that point can do."

Is there maintenance involved with the burning tool? He said that with the older-style, brass-tipped pen, the buildup of wood was considerable. But with the newer steel points, there is little if any buildup of wood residue. "But if you do have to touch them up, you don't need a file. Just sand lightly with #400 wet/dry sandpaper."

I asked him what setting he will burn at, or does he go to different settings for different areas to be burned? "The settings on the rheostat are not always accurate because some of these pens are hotter than others and some points have different consistencies of hardness," he replied. "I've found that the hardness or type of steel has a lot to do with how hot the point gets. But you almost have to experiment with each pen and its points."

Jim did not equivocate on the next issue, and he is the only carver I have heard say this: "It's important to use the burning pen so that you have the least amount of resistance with the cord. You obviously don't have the freedom of movement if you feel it pulling. If there were a burning pen that didn't have a cord, I would go for that. I just don't want the tail wagging the dog."

In spite of the cord, Jim would seem to have no trouble burning barb lines and even the outlines of feathers. He explained that after he defined the back's

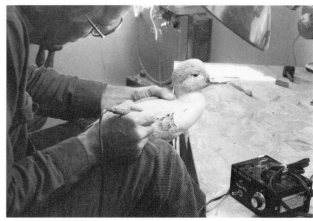

The burning of the gadwall body begins on the side pockets. Here Jim uses the Detailer, manufactured by Colwood Electronics (see Appendix for address).

scapular features with an X-acto or carver's knife, he took the burning pen and redefined them, much as he did with cuts made on the bill, "My burning pen point drops right down into that stop cut. And this will help me when it comes time to take my chisel and start relieving some of those feathers because of that track I've created. That chisel just falls into that little crease. It gives a lot of accuracy. Perhaps I just stumbled onto this method."

Flicking Burning Lines

Jim uses a flicking wrist action in his burning technique. Perhaps this is a result of his having been a

Going back over the stoning lines with the burning pen gives the illusions, Jim says, of feathers at different levels or depths. With the pen, he can also burn in feather splits.

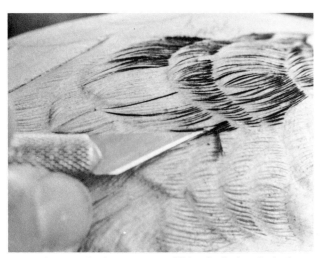

Using the X-acto knife, Jim can cut additional splits into the feathers.

baseball pitcher. But before he would elaborate, he told me that he burns additional lines at the base of the quills. "It's tighter there, with more strands of feathers at the shaft. Doing this gives the appearance of more hair."

"Burning is very monotonous," he added. "I've noticed so many carvers who have only hours or weekends to do birds, so when it comes to burning, they hurry through it. And burning is something you cannot hurry. All those thousands of lines are very deliberate. So you have to be resigned to the fact that it's going to take time. It's *so* important to the end result."

How much time does he spend burning? On some days he puts in 12 to 14 hours, he said. "Talk about monotony. But after a day, you can really see what you've accomplished."

When Jim got around to answering my question about flicking burning lines, he explained that "Some carvers burn too stiff, too straight. Feathers really have a little twist. That's what I'm doing when I burn. Also, those same carvers make the feather as heavily burned at the base as at the tip. This is wrong. I guess it's because those carvers can't burn finely enough."

I asked him how hot he made the burning pen, despite the differences in metal tips, and whether more or less heat made a difference in the burn. "I think I have a tendency to burn hot," he said. "Yet, the hotter the point, the faster the burning goes. This may seem like a contradiction, since I don't advocate speed when burning, though we're not talking about a great deal of difference in time. I guess it's a tradeoff. Because if the point is cooler, the end result may be a

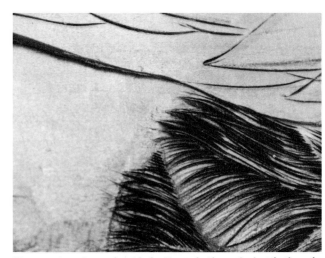

Here are the splits made with the X-acto knife on the last feather of a side pocket.

Painting Instructions for the Gadwall Drake

A good shot showing the colors on the crown of the head. The forehead is cream to off-white, the crown is a shade of burnt sienna and burnt umber mix, and the back to hind neck is almost black. Always check reference for the flow of feathers coming off the head and neck onto the chest, and for the shape and size of the chest feathers.

Note shape of upper and lower mandibles, and look closely at your study bills before carving. Study the blackish streak on face feather pattern, usually lighter in color directly behind the bill and under chin. Gadwall's nostrils are much closer to face than those of most other ducks. Also notice the three different colors on the crown.

In painting the gadwall, one of the hardest areas is the transition from the breast feathers to the front portion of the side pocket feathers. When painting this area, be sure your base colors are correct. The breast is almost jet black while the side pockets have more of a brownish cast. Use a Langnickle series 671 #0 or a red sable brush with black to split up the white breast feathers.

Use a white lead pencil to lay out feathers lightly before painting. Try to show color of the wing coverts and secondaries. Check reference (hopefully a study skin or mount) to determine where the three colors stop and start.

First row of scapulars have the same gray color as the leading edges of the tertials. Quills are a medium brown. Study the transition of vermiculation from back area to the scapular feathers. Sprankle uses a Strathmore Kolinsky #2 on all vermiculating and puts a few coats of matte-medium on the quills to create a slight gloss. Note the green cast of the inside portion of the primary feathers.

Scapular feather laying over the tertials. Notice the feather splits on the gray tertial feathers and the small area of black between side pockets and scapulars, which is the black area on the wing coverts. Photo also shows a small portion of the thigh.

A gadwall drake usually has a green shade on the upper and under tail coverts. Before painting this green area, lightly flick yellow ochre on the feather tips. If you're using acrylic paints, this procedure is important. Photo also shows the different shades of color on the tail area with the edges of the feathers showing white.

The gadwall drake has a distinct shape to his rump. The under surface of the primaries has the same value of gray shades as the tail, with a whitish quill on the under part of the primary feather.

A good shot of the rump with the green color on the upper and under tail coverts. Note the burning technique used in this area. Burn the tertial and scapular feathers as close as possible. Remember the cooler the point of the burning pen, the closer you'll be able to put individual strokes. Don't hurry!

Don't overlook vermiculation under the rump and directly behind the side pockets. Note splits in speculum where the dark color of the sides can show. The adult gadwall drake will have four tertial feathers, with the lower one showing a darker shade. These tertial feathers have a fine white edging and their tips have a whitish cast, with a faint color of raw sienna on the quills.

A History of Sprankle Ducks

Goldeneye hen. 1971

Bluebill drake. 1973

Black duck drake. 1974

Wood duck drake. 1975

Widgeon drake. 1976

Shoveler drake. 1977

Hooded merganser drake. 1978

Green-winged teal drake. 1979

Harlequin drake. 1980

Ruddy duck drake. *1981*

Canvasback drake. 1982

Bufflehead drake. 1983

Hooded merganser hen. 1984

Black duck drake. 1985

Ruddy duck drake. *1984*

First place in specie, World Championship.

Photo by J. D. Sprankle.

Bufflehead drake. *1984*

Second place in specie, World Championship.

Photo by J. D. Sprankle.

Gadwall drake. *1984*
First place in specie, World Championship.
Photo by J. D. Sprankle.

Canvasback drake. *1983*
Photo by J. D. Sprankle.

Ringneck drake. *1984*

First place in specie, World Championship.

Photo by J. D. Sprankle.

Shoveler drake. *1984*

First place in specie, World Championship.

Photo by J. D. Sprankle.

Cinnamon teal drake. 1984

Ruddy duck pair. 1985
Photo by J. D. Sprankle.

The left side pocket has been burned as has the right side and top. Note that the quill lines, burned in but with the pen angled over, do not line up.

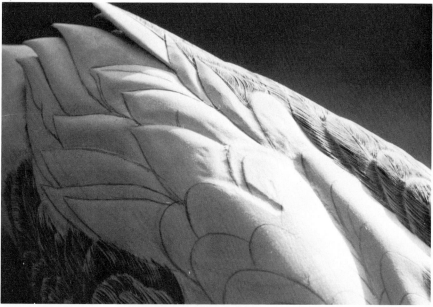

The same area from a different angle shows the encroaching burning lines of barbs and quills on the relieved back.

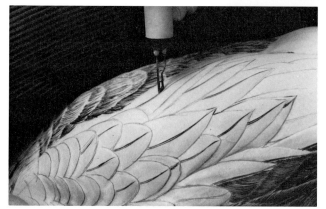

Jim demonstrates burning in the quills with the pen laid over to one side.

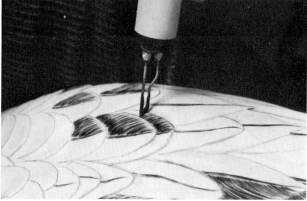

For the barbs, however, he burns vertically for thinner lines and therefore more lines per inch.

Here the side pocket of the cinnamon teal has been burned. The area in the middle has not been, because the thrust-forward leg will be attached there.

This photo details the burning on the breast.

little bit better. You see, a hot tip will, though minutely, break down the strength of the wood left between the burning lines. This gives the wood less body. If you're burning cooler, I think you can get your lines a little closer together."

But with the quill lines, Jim said that he did indeed use less heat than for the barb lines. "Since they're so fine, I find that I have more control with less heat. Also, I tip the pen at about a forty-five degree angle

which sort of rounds those quills over. And when you're ready to paint, you can round them over even more by taking a fine brush and building up the quills with gesso. It sure makes them look more realistic."

Does Jim have a particular burning strategy, a place on the duck where he begins? "I like to start my burning from the front and work backward. I do that in case I burn into the next feather. If I do, I can always cover it up. But if I started from the back, with this

A final photo showing the burning lines on the right side.

The back of the gadwall is completely burned. Study the flow of the quills and barb lines as well as the layout of the feathers that avoid a scaly appearance.

Back to the gadwall, you can observe how the right side was burned. Jim will first burn the side away from the turned head. This, he feels, gives him a feel for the burning, or perhaps a fluency, before he proceeds to the side that will be looked at more.

Another technique Jim uses is to do all the burning on one side of the quills and then on the other. This keeps him from having to turn the bird around in his hand after each half feather is done.

After burning the gadwall's sides and back, Jim cleans away wood from underneath the tertials with a long-bladed carver's knife. What cannot be seen is the Wilton power vise the bird is mounted on. Also, for demonstration purposes, only half the bird was burned at this stage.

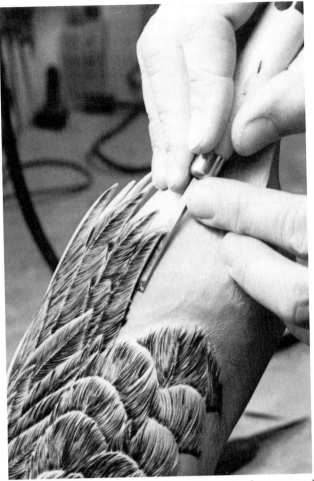

A chisel also reaches underneath the tertial area to clean out wood where the primaries will be inserted.

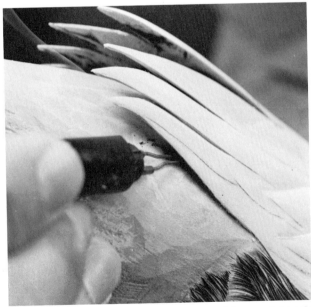

The burning pen is used here to burn away wood fuzz created by the knife and chisel work in the previous steps.

Jim's X-acto knife cuts out an area between two tertials to accept the primaries.

loose-wrist method of burning I use, I would end up dragging the pen over into the preceding feather. So at the end of a feather, where I've made a finer thinner line with my loose wrist, it's not difficult to cover up a line that got too long."

He said he had yet another strategy when burning. "I like to do the right-hand side first if the bird's head is turned to the left [remember that when a bird faces to the observer's left, the person should look at that side of the body]. The reason is, you get the flow of things going on one side and get it right. Then you can go the the other side that people will be looking at more."

There was one more strategy to his burning that perhaps few would notice unless it was pointed out to them. Jim is very careful to burn with a perpendicular pen. "As soon as you tip the pen to one side, you're creating a wider line," and he wants as many fine lines as he can achieve.

Nubbins

It was early afternoon by the time Jim had burned his way to the tail area on the unburned side, leaving untouched only the space where the primaries would be inserted. But before he continued, he would shape what he called the nubbins.

I checked F. W. Kortwright's *Ducks, Geese, and Swans of North America*, a book nearly all professional carvers refer to for waterfowl information, on the correct anatomical term. There was nothing I could find that seemed quite right, but the nubbins appeared to

Before finishing up the tail area by defining and burning its feathers, Jim proceeds on to the leg stubs he calls nubbins, which have become a trademark of his work. he starts with a ⅜-inch-thick piece of basswood and a template. Shaping of the cutout is done with his cone-shaped, double-cut bit.

An added touch of Jim's is putting in the scales on these diminutive legs with a gouge held with its cutting edge down.

A ruby carver puts in more definition, forming the basic structure of the nubbin.

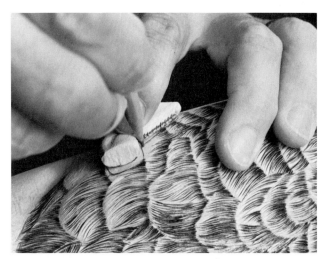

When the legs are finished, they are located on the body near the flat bottom.

be the upper parts of the legs. These Jim would carve and attach to the sides of the gadwall.

From a pattern and a three-eighths-inch-thick piece of basswood, Jim quickly shaped these tiny pieces with different grinders. When the Foredom wasn't running, he said, "I put on these leg stumps because I believe you can see this part of the bird even when it's in the water. They've become a trademark of mine, though other carvers put them on from time to time. The bottom line is, they add more realism and I get comments that people 'love those little legs.' To some degree, you have to carve what people want. And if they're put on right they're neat."

His double-cut bit makes a depression to receive the nubbin.

The legs are then glued with Devcon epoxy and slight pressure.

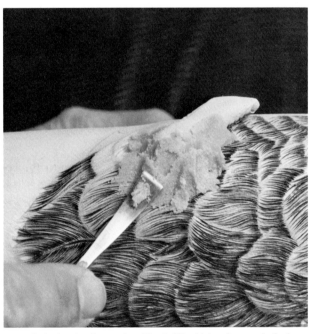

With the legs in place, 3-in-1 Plastic Wood joins them to the body.

As with the eyes, neck, and the rear part of the bill, the Plastic Wood has been worked and feathered with solvent and chisel.

On some birds, Jim attaches the entire webbed feet. This one is on a full-bodied gadwall drake.

On the flat-bottomed black duck, Jim has also put an entire leg and foot. This leg was made from two pieces of basswood and feathered into the body with Plastic Wood.

Before putting on individual feathers, Jim cleans up the undertail. He says to note the shape here since it is a distinctive feature of a gadwall.

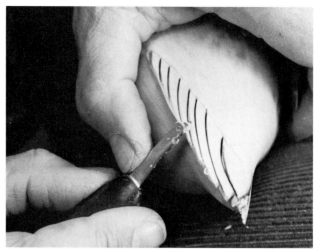

Before chiseling, he shapes the tips of the feathers.

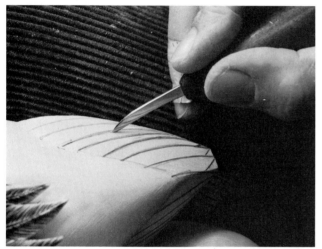

A knife traces the tail feather separations Jim has drawn on to create grooves.

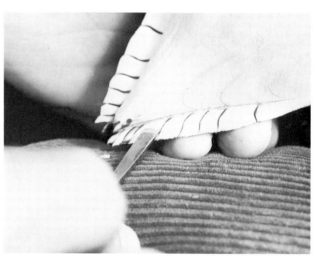

Underneath, he relieves the feathers so that they overlap.

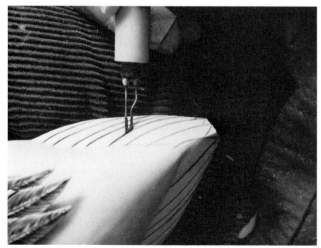

The burning pen redefines the individual tail feathers, creating a larger groove for the chisel.

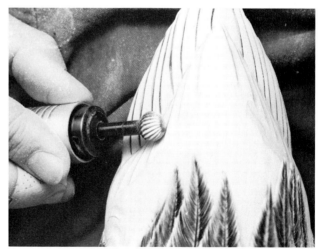

Next, with this ball-shaped cutter, Jim defines feather groupings on the upper tail area before burning.

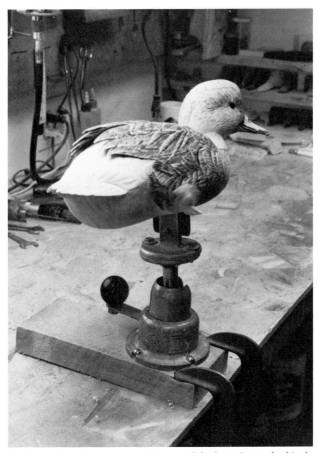

Finally, he is ready to separate the top tail feathers. But to do this, he must have both hands free, so he again mounts the gadwall on the power vise. Note the depressions just above the base of the tail.

Jim will, of course, go farther and add webbed feet to his full-bodied birds, ones that extend out into imaginary water. But he rarely carves standing ducks. "To make them right, the duck almost has to be involved in a scene. You have to make water and grass and other habitat. That's a job for someone like John Scheeler, not me."

A short time after bandsawing these nubbins to shape, Jim was ready to apply them to the duck, using

Both hands now guide a small chisel to lower each adjoining feather slightly, starting from the middle and working toward each side.

Finished, the results of layering can be studied.

his two-part Devcon epoxy as the gluing agent. Then, after having made a slight cavity on the sides of the duck so the nubbins would not project out too far, the leg stumps and body were joined with Plastic Wood.

After the Plastic Wood had set, Jim would burn in feather details. But he would also burn the nubbin, making parallelograms formed by crosshatching lines. Into each of those he would put a drop of gesso. This would give the stumps their scaly appearance.

Before we broke for dinner at 5:30, Jim said he was anxious to detail the tail feathers. "I don't like to thin the tail down to its actual carving size to soon," he said, "because it becomes fragile and therefore vulnerable. So after most of the other work has been completed, I

Here the area around the leg that had Plastic Wood applied has to be burned. Jim first draws in the feathers.

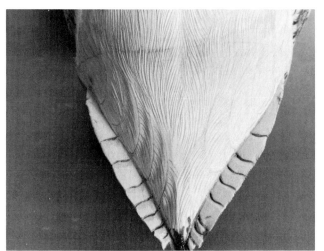

The underside of the tail is stoned.

After the Plastic Wood is burned, crosshatching lines are burned onto the nubbins to simulate the scaly look on their sides. Into each square he will later put a drop of gesso, a thick primer for acrylics, to make the scales stand out.

This photo details the tail area and upper rump completely stoned and burned. Note the twists in the burning lines, a technique Jim has mastered to give his ducks more realism.

The under-rump area and the leg details can be studied here.

The wooden primary feathers of this gadwall are made from templates taken from a live bird. There are ten on a wing, but Jim cuts out only four or five. Those that he is outlining with a knife are made from tupelo gum, a wood native to Louisiana, though he usually utilizes basswood for these feathers.

thin it down before I start to put in details." He does this using a knife to sculpt it thinner, then reliefing the individual feathers with knife, burning pen, and chisel. When finished, he would then stone and burn in details between the tail and undercut tertials as well as the rump or under-tail anatomy. This and the shaping and detailing of the primaries would be completed before the evening (and my second visit) was over.

Primary Inserts

Here would be the only place Jim would use tupelo gum on the gadwall – as primary feather inserts. Why? "Because I had some on hand, but I don't really see an advantage over basswood." He had cut thin pieces of it on the tablesaw, some no more than one-sixteenth-inch thick.

The templates for the primaries came from his reference envelope. These he transferred to the wood and cut out the outlines with a carver's knife. But the tupelo feathers were still not thin enough. He went to his pneumatic sanding drum and ground or "buffed" away more wood, leaving the feathers only one-thirty-second- or even one-sixty-fourth-inch thick.

Two-part epoxy held the feathers together, but Jim used an additional trick. While the glue was drying, he was bending the feather groupings to give them the proper curvature. One final step was to apply Wonder Bond to the tips of these primary groupings. "It makes the wood just like metal," he said.

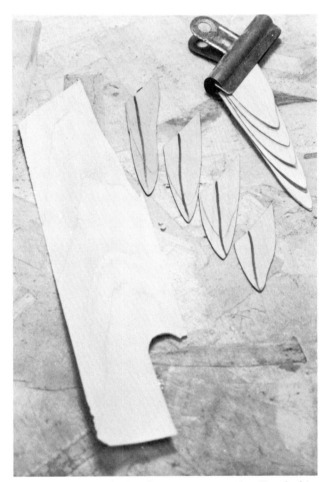

In the clip are the five feathers for one primary grouping. Note the faint pencil lines on the individual feathers. Jim traces the overlays on the lower ones to insure that the feathers are not reversed when glued in place.

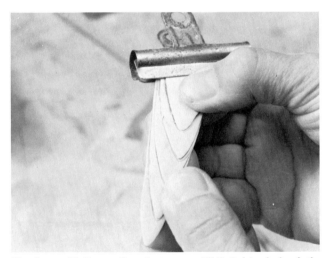

The glue used is Devcon five-minute epoxy. While it dries, he bends the grouping to achieve a slight curve in the feathers.

Avoiding Damage

I had heard many stories of carvings being damaged in transit and even at shows. One carver I knew even got on a plane to deliver a pair of birds personally. When I saw how delicate the primary tips looked, I asked Jim how he avoided breaking them. He said that when shipping a bird to a show or customer, he would first put the duck in a soft cloth bag and "float" it in Styrofoam pellets in a large cardboard poultry box, a stiff and waterproof container. "I haven't had too many casualties. But I will have an occasional wingtip broken. It's the nature of what we're doing. You have much more of a problem with the bigger

This is a detail of a burned primary grouping.

Jim now predetermines how much of the primary groupings have to be burned.

Here can be seen how the primary groupings come off the body.

Burning can now be done on the groupings. Note that he has put the quill lines in first and does not have to start at the very base of the first feather. Jim also points out that this same pen can be used to scrape away excess glue from the wood that would later interfere with painting.

Before proceeding to the painting, Jim adds a final touch to the gadwall—the wrinkles or creases on the upper mandible. For these he uses as hard a pencil lead as he can, a No. 9. When covered with paint, the pencil marks will vanish, leaving only thin crevices.

decorative pieces." He added that he ships all his birds via United Parcel Service with few problems, but is careful to pack them well. "Few things are as frustrating as repairing a bird. I guess it's like doing artist's remarques. After a while, it's not very creative."

Scraping with Heat and Bill Crevices

Before Jim would insert these groupings into the back of the gadwall, he first burned in quills and barbs, reminding me that quills are done with a low heat intensity. He also said, as the feathers darkened, that he could remove dried epoxy with the tip of the heated burning pen, "scraping it off with heat."

But he still would not insert the feathers until they and the gadwall had been completely painted. They would get in the way, he said, and could just as easily be painted separately.

Jim felt the evening would not be complete without adding a final detail to the bill. On many ducks' bills there are wrinkles, crevices really, around the nostrils and the base of the bill. But they cannot be burned in

because they are wider than the burning pen tip. To re-create these crevices, Jim uses "about the hardest pencil lead that can be bought, a No. 9." When painted, however, the unrealistic pencil marks will disappear.

Room for Improvement?

I asked Jim, before we returned to the house, what improvements he has made during his nine years of professional carving. "I've gone through different plateaus, and I've made all the mistakes that can be made. My bodies were too square, my eye positioning was not good, my bill detail wasn't what it should be," he said.

"I guess the bottom line for the top ten percent of the carvers today is accuracy. Before we just didn't have the reference available we have now. And the more you preach about it, the more you pick it up. Still, I wonder whether some of the better carvers can get very much more accurate. But there's always room for improvement here and there."

5

Water Blending, Flicking Feathers, and the Art of Painting

Getting Started

As I traveled south to Maryland for our last session with the gadwall, I thought about the question I hear most often asked by carvers at home, at shows, and at clubs I attend. What are the secrets of painting? they ask. How do you paint this bird you have carved? I myself once tried painting, and was surprised to learn that no matter how I mixed my acrylics, I could not create the colors I wanted. Many of those same carvers ask me when I will do a book devoted solely to painting birds, perhaps with many brightly colored photos. One carver even suggested something reminiscent of the color-by-number technique.

I had reviewed my notes from the last visit. It was when Jim was shaping the primary feathers that he had spoken about the gadwall being a painter's challenge. "You have some things going on a gadwall that are key in making the thing look right. One of the things is simple, though it doesn't sound simple, and that's the transition from the definite breast patterns of little cups to the vermiculation on the sides. I guess

that's why there's never been a lot of carvings of this bird. It's so difficult to paint, and, until more recently, there was less reference available." He had pointed to one of the two gadwall study mounts he uses. "Look at those streak patterns on the face. That's another thing that has to be captured."

The morning he started painting the gadwall was a bright one, almost too bright, for the water reflected sunlight off the bay and up through the windows of his painting room. On the plywood benchtop was the gessoed bird, more ghost than gadwall. And true to his reliance on reference, Jim had open on that workbench a notebook containing painting notes not only for the gadwall, but also for 24 other birds he has carved and painted since 1976. These notes and patterns comprise chapter 6.

The notes divide the bird into areas of the head, the rump, the sides, breast, long and short back feathers, speculum, tail, wings, bill, and legs. The birds are titled with the year the notes were taken. Some have revisions, also dated, and most of his notes are abbreviated. And in the margins of many pages are swat-

Jim's painting room is separated from the carving area to minimize dust and clutter. At the far left is a corkboard that will hold pinups of birds he can study while carving or painting. In the upper right is his slide projector used for making patterns.

The Badger HD (heavy duty) 150 airbrush Jim uses for "skim" coats of watered down acrylics or for a softening effect on already applied colors. But too much airbrushing on a bird, he warns, can result in a ceramic look.

The open-top cup is what holds the acrylic paint. He says that a ratio of seven parts water to three parts acrylic paint is probably best. He also advises mixing the water and paint in the cup thoroughly as he is doing here.

ches of acrylic colors, perhaps to trigger his memory of a color mix, for Jim admitted that these dabs of dried color are not very accurate.

Much of what follows is a verbatim account of Jim's painting techniques as the gadwall progressed from a stark white to a vermiculated duck. But it was a tense time for Jim, made difficult by doing this species. Even his always-turned-on radio was lower in volume than usual. And I do not think Jim was accustomed to having someone standing so close to him, making him stop his painting strokes for camera stills. But as he worked, he would suspend painting and comment on what he was doing, often repeating my questions, even repeating himself. By the end of that weekend, I had learned a painting vocabulary, picking up terms such as feather flicking, vermiculating, Hooker's green, and blending color to water.

The Badger HD150

When we started that Saturday morning, Jim was busy not with mixing paints but with cleaning an airbrush, starting and stopping the attached compressor. "If you don't keep the airbrush clean after each use, you're going to ruin it very quickly," he said. "It will plug up all the time.

"I use a Badger HD150 with three different nozzles and I use all three. This HD gives more of an overall spray effect. But any time you use acrylics in an airbrush, you want to really water down the paint. If it's the least bit thick, you'll plug up the nozzle.

"Now I'm not going to airbrush the whole bird. In fact, airbrushing is something I don't advocate, because I think some people learn to take the path of least resistance, and they use it more often than they should. When you do that, there's no way you can hide the airbrush look. I know a very well-known carver who went wild with an airbrush. Soon, all his carvings looked the same, ceramic almost. Be careful using it; pick your places for it. I'll tell you that it's not quicker, so that theory is out. I use it mostly on bills. There are some bills I can't pull off otherwise. But I'll put what I call a skim coat on tertials. What it does is soften the look just a bit. Or put another way, you airbrush until you get the right intensity of color.

"Do you have to hold the airbrush a certain distance from the bird? You almost have to play that by eye. I'd say three to six inches. But if you want a narrower line, of course you have to get closer. If you want an overall spray, the farther back you can get, the better."

"I'll airbrush the final coat to soften the look of the washes I've applied. Especially for a bird like the gadwall, it gives a softer, subtler look. It seems to even up the washes already applied."

But the airbrush sometimes has a companion tool, he pointed out. "I'll airbrush with a hairdryer blowing a stream of hot air. The paint dries almost on impact, alleviating its running, which is going to happen if too much is applied."

Preparing the Bird

"I put on about three thin coats of Deft, a maple-colored spray called Salem Maple Stain. This I do before gessoing the bird. The maple color seems to leave the wood in its most natural color. Also, it's a lacquer, so I use it to seal the wood. Since gesso is a water base, it will fuzz up the wood unless it's sealed. All this goes back to cleaning up the wood as I did with sandpaper and steel wool.

"Then I take gesso and mix a little bit of raw umber with it, and I put two coats of the mix on top of the Deft, which gives me a base on which to paint.

"I use a stiff bristle brush, a Windsor & Newton brush with short bristles about an inch wide. If it isn't stiff it doesn't force the gesso down into the textured areas.

"I work a little harder around the areas with plastic wood, the eyes, the neck, and the leg nubbins to get them sealed properly. They take a little more sealant to blend them with the existing wood.

"How long does it take for gesso to dry? That has a lot to do with its consistency when it's put on and the room temperature. I would say about five minutes. But I don't advise using a hairdryer, as I use with the acrylics, to dry gesso. I've noticed that if gesso dries too quickly, it leaves pinholes or craters down in the burned grooves. It took me a long time to figure out what was happening when I used the hairdryer. So when using a stiff brush to apply gesso, always go with the flow of the burned feathers. If you put it on perpendicular to the feather flow, when it dries, you'll have brush marks you can't get out."

Mixing on Glass

"I feel it's important to mix my colors on glass with something white underneath like paper towels because I have a better idea of how the colors will look on gesso.

A way to keep the airbrush paint from running on the bird is to use a hairdryer at the same time. This will dry the water and paint mix almost instantly. Here he sprays a thin wash of burnt umber over the vermiculated areas to soften or tone down the white.

A spray stain called Deft first seals the wood on the gadwall. Then gesso, a thick white primer that offers a base for acrylics, is applied.

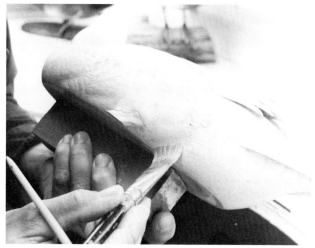

Jim demonstrates how he applies gesso with a stiff brush, working the paint with the texturing so that all areas are filled.

Acrylics are mixed on glass with a white paper towel underneath. The white, he feels, simulates the gesso, so he can tell how the mix will look on the bird before actually applying it.

Acrylics must be mixed with water or they would be too thick to apply. He makes what are called washes on the glass, and he may have to apply as many as seven to get the right color intensity. This is a mix of titanium white, gesso, and raw umber for the head, lower sides, and rump.

Caps from the Deft spray stain cover or "cap" the mixes to preserve them and keep them from drying up. With a little moisture added to the inside of the cap, the mix will keep a couple of days.

To remove a hardening acrylic mix, a shortened putty knife can scrape the glass clean.

"How do I know about the consistency? If you're mixing paint and your end result is shiny, or filling up the texturing marks, it's too thick. My philosophy is, there's no way to put it on too thin. So the bottom line is, put it on thin and build it up.

"Also, when putting these mixes of water and acrylics on, when you go back to your pallet, or piece of glass in my case, it's always a good idea to stir it around a little. They do have a tendency to separate a bit. This way, you'll get a better, more even color.

"Also, I use Deft plastic lids to cap my colors and keep them from drying out. I believe in saving these mixes as long as I can because they're not easy to duplicate if you have to do some touching up. And it's a good idea to put a little moisture from your brush into that cap. That helps slow down the drying time.

"Another thing I use is a regular putty knife cut off and sharpened to scrape the glass."

Windsor & Newton

"You asked me about these Windsor & Newton brushes I use (the address is in the Appendix). They're red sable brushes, made by a London-based firm, and they're not easy to find. A lot of dealers won't buy them because they cost so much. Synthetic brushes work well too, I'm told. But it all goes back to what you're used to using."

Painting Keel

"You probably noticed that I put a keel on the bird. I use it to keep my fingers off it. It's a wooden handle, nothing more. Two drops of five-minute epoxy keep it stuck on so that I don't physically have to handle the bird any more than is absolutely necessary. Especially in the summer, sweat and oil on your hands get on the bird, and paint won't stick. But if paint should not stick for some reason, I spray on Windex. The ammonia in it and a paper towel will cut away the grease.

"To remove the keel, I tap it with a hammer. But if you have too much glue and too much hammer, you may jar loose the plate plug."

Mixing Colors

"So you ask how someone arrives at color mixes? Some stagger onto them, but we've all had help with these things. The guy who says he learned everything on his own is pulling your leg.

"I can tell people the exact mix I use, but that doesn't mean they're going to come up with the same color I do, for the same reason you can't tell someone how many washes to apply. At some point it's left up to your trained eye to evaluate colors. I don't think you can train anyone at this.

"Painting, then, is obviously the hardest thing. But why, I'm not really sure. Painting classes and seminars are really going to help with this.

"You know, I believe painting is eighty percent of the end result in this field. It sures helps cover up a multitude of sins. A well-carved bird with a poor paint job is not likely to do well in competition. On the other hand, a bird that is not carved so well but has a good paint job is pretty tough to beat. So I think a person should try to concentrate on the painting. It will pay dividends.

"As for washes, I can tell you it's very hard to tell someone how many to put on a bird, for rarely will two people mix the same consistencies of water and acrylics. So you just can't say it takes two or three or whatever number of washes. You'll see in my painting notes that only occasionally do I refer to numbers of washes."

The First Washes

"I put on the paint for the upper two-thirds, the back and the breast. The breast has a definitely darker cast than the sides, which have a brownish-black color. The mix I use to get the color on the sides and back is an ultramarine blue and a burnt sienna. You can get a lot of different shades out of these two col-

This one-inch-wide sable brush, made by Windsor & Newton (see Appendix for address), is used to apply the washes on various areas of the bird.

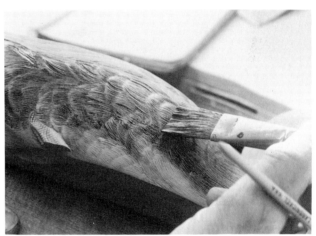

With his Windsor & Newton brush, Jim applies the first wash of ultramarine blue and burnt sienna for the brown shade.

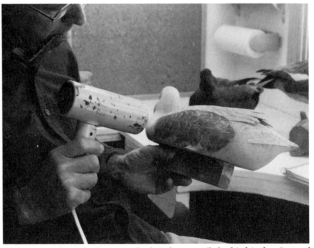

Between each wash, Jim uses the hairdryer until the bird is dry. Instead of testing the paint with his fingers, he holds the bird up against his cheek.

The side pocket of the gadwall increases in its color value as the fourth wash is applied.

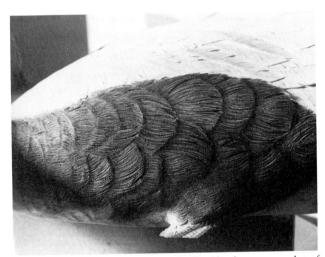

And here is the appearance of the gadwall's side after seven washes of burnt umber and ultramarine blue were put on.

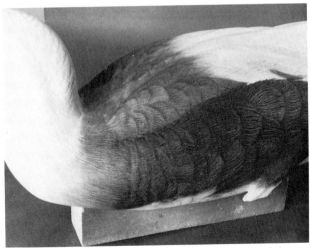

The short back feathers behind the neck will also be a mix of ultramarine blue and burnt sienna. Note that the mix does not extend into the scapular feathers.

The number of mixes for the back is the same as for the sides. But Jim did not do the back at the same time as the sides in order to avoid what he calls "an acrylic runoff," resulting from too much paint being applied at one time.

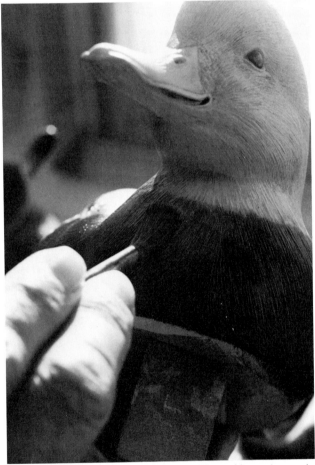

The breast is a darker shade of ultramarine blue and burnt sienna mix, with more ultramarine blue to make the wash darker.

ors. In fact, I make all my brown and black shades from this mix. So don't ever use straight black. If you want a black shade, use more ultramarine blue.

"To get the best shades of black and brown, I use Grumbacher's Hyplar. I've tried Liquitex and Aquatec, but they result in a purplish color. Still, I use some Liquitex for other mixes. I really like the Mars black and the titanium white of the Liquitex brand. Their colors don't seem to separate nearly as much as the Hyplar colors when mixing on glass with water.

"My guess is that it will take four or five washes of this ultramarine blue and burnt sienna mix." It took seven washes to achieve the density of color Jim wanted.

"Now when the top two-thirds of the gadwall are dry, I'll blend it to the bottom third. If left wet, the two will run together instead of blending."

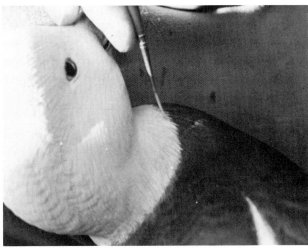

Feather edges can be lost when washes are applied. Here Jim cuts these in with a mix of gesso, titanium white, and raw umber, using a No. 1 Langnickel brush.

Blending Color to Water

"One thing you have to master when working with acrylics is blending color to water. In my opinion, the rest comes easy if you can do that – at least it did for me.

"Blending, basically, is a situation in which you paint the lighter color of two adjoining areas, dampening that area, but not real wet, then take the next darker color and blend the two together. This method should fuse the colors together as if they were oils.

"This doesn't just come because you want it to. But when you get the feel for blending color to water, you're dealing with something that people say can't be blended, acrylics that is. If done right, you get a nice soft transition from one color to another. If you didn't do this, you'd get a hard line where the new color went on.

"When blending color to water, if you get too much water on the bird, it will roll onto the area where you want to paint, and right away the consistency of the mix will change.

"Originally, stipling or pushing down with a brush compensated for the hard lines. Old-timers working on decoys did this. But there are some areas of this gadwall where there will be hard lines, like where the speculum and the side meet. I think this lends to the beauty of the bird.

"Another thing when blending, I keep two cannisters of clean water handy so that I can keep my brush perfectly clean."

A small brush dampens an area to be left white or off-white. The darker brown wash will fuse with the water, eliminating a hard line. This is what Jim calls blending color to water.

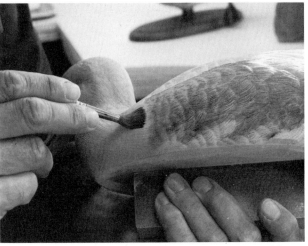

He also dampens or "waters in" an area where the breast will have a different color or shade. He waters this area before each wash of ultramarine blue and burnt sienna.

Jim dampens yet another light area, as washes of the brownish mix are applied above it.

Here Jim is mixing paint on glass. In front of him is a study mount of a gadwall drake. The natural light from outside can be an important aid to painting the correct color values. Consequently, he has combined cool, warm, and special refrigeration fluorescent bulbs to achieve what will appear like natural light inside the painting room.

Drying the Washes

"I don't just slop paint on. I really try to define areas. But what also helps is the hairdryer between successive washes.

"How do I know the paint is dry? I lay the bird up against my cheek because I hate to touch it with my fingers. It's very important before you put that next wash on that the previous one is dry, because if it isn't, it will pull the previous coat off. Then you'll have a measled-looking paint job.

"Also, I try to do groupings of feathers, four at a time, then three, then back to four. I do this so I don't get paint running over everything, and it gives the watery mix a chance to disperse."

Fresh Mounts and Tethered Ducks

"When painting, I think it's important to get clean, fresh mounts or study skins. As you can see, I use two.

"I've even brought a live bird into the studio. I remember a redhead drake I'd tether and set on a two-foot square piece of cardboard. Occasionally, when I'm painting a bird, I may bring it in and hold it behind its wings, and take a knife and pallette and mix my colors and compare them to the live bird.

"When I compare the two study mounts I have in front of me, it's obvious that one has darker tertials. In fact, the whole bird is darker. So when judging, it's pretty hard to tell someone his bird is too dark or too light unless the bird's values are really off.

"Still, there's no opportunity in the carving world to take liberties when painting a bird. It's so cut and

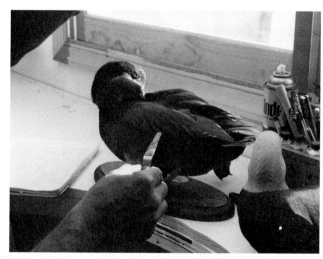

With painting notes before him and a good study mount, Jim compares his color mix to the gadwall.

dried that the bird has to be lifelike. So when I'm judging, for example, I have to ask myself how much the bird looks like the one I see in my aviary."

The Tertials

"After I get a base coat on the breast and sides, and a dark portion on the back and up toward the head, the next feathers to be painted are what I call the smoke feathers, the gray tertials. To get the gray, I use a white base with small amounts of burnt umber and black, with a bit more burnt umber than black. Then I water those into the feathers that have a golden cast.

"I'll use the airbrush and put a skim coat on the tertials after that. It softens the look just a bit."

The Quills

"For the quills, I use a very light coat or two of raw sienna, watered down so it doesn't come off with a gold color. You know, it's easier to start and stop while carving than it is to paint and talk and get a fine line at the same time. You almost have to hold your breath."

The Scapulars

"For these, I use a mix of raw sienna base with small amounts of white, burnt umber, and burnt sienna. The centers of the feathers are a mix of burnt umber and a small amount of white. Then I flick a white and raw umber mix on the tips.

"The raw umber takes the starkness out of the

Even though it is black and white, this photo should give an idea of the contrasting density of colors on the mount, especially of the tertials.

The first wash on the tertials is a combination of white and small amounts of burnt umber and black.

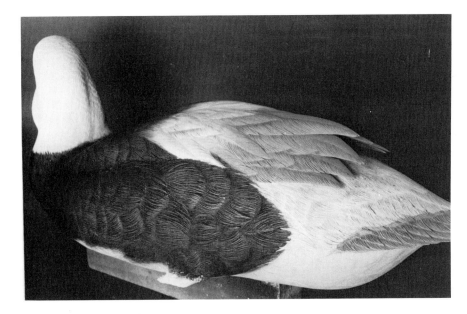

In this photo the difference in color intensity between the sides and tertials can be seen.

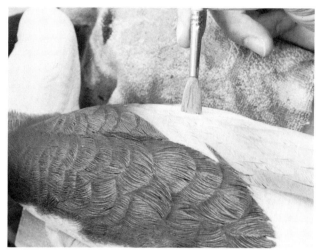

Jim waters in the area behind the tertials.

To highlight the quills, Jim uses a fine brush and a watery mix of raw sienna.

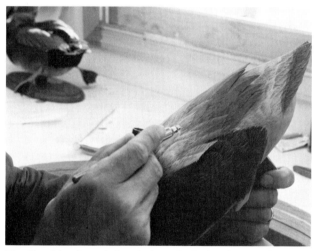

Here Jim airbrushes a darker shade on the feathers between the tertials and scapulars. This is a mix of white, burnt umber, and black, with more of the latter two paints to darken the color.

The scapulars begin as a mix of raw sienna base with small amounts of white, burnt umber, and burnt sienna. Then he blends in their centers with a mix of burnt umber and a small amount of white.

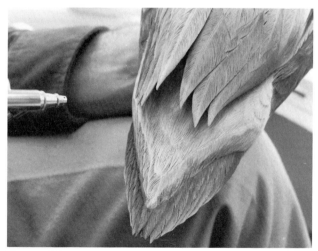

The tips of the tertials are airbrushed with white and a small amount of raw umber.

Here is the final blending of the scapular centers. The quills are two watery washes of burnt umber.

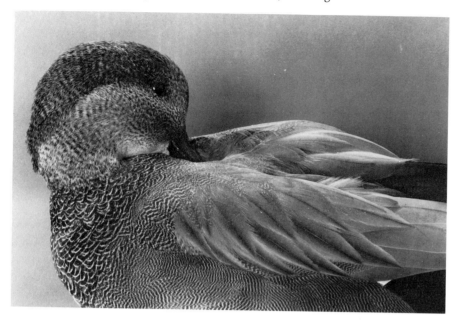

For comparison note the scapulars on his study mount.

white. John Scheeler told me about this mix years ago, and it's the best piece of advice I ever got."

Flicking Feather Tips

"There's one other thing you have to master, besides blending to water, and that's flicking feather tips.

"Feather tips, particularly on hens, have distinct, defined edges. So I use a mixture of titanium white and raw umber. That whitish base will accept whatever other wash is applied over it. Those other washes will tone down the white, but will still leave a subtle yet defined edge.

"So you have to put the white on first. This goes back to understanding acrylics. If everything is properly applied, the white will reflect through. But you can't put a dark color on a dark color and achieve anything.

"Flicking feather tips does not come the first day you try it. The key is having the right combination in your mix of water to paint, and not having your brush too wet. It's got to be dry enough so that when you fan your brush open to create the feather edges, you will get that shape. I use, then, a brush that stays fanned open."

Under and Above the Tail

"These areas are almost a jet black. So I use about a two-to-one mixture of ultramarine blue to burnt si-

A closeup shows the completed back.

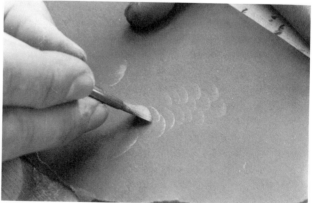

Jim demonstrates on paper the flicking of feather tips. For this he must use a brush with its hairs fanned out.

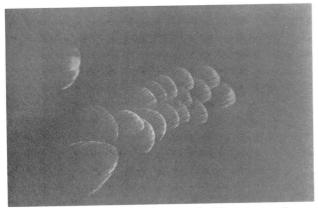

A closeup shows the effect of flicking with white and raw umber.

The under-rump is painted with a mix of ultramarine blue and burnt sienna with a small amount of Mars black.

enna. It's a liquidy black, not a Mars black that would give the look of patent-leather shoes.

"If you look at the study mounts, you'll see that right behind the tail feathers on the top side there's a greenish cast. You have to look closely to pick it up. For this I use a Hooker's green and black mix. I then paint the feather tips with a yellow ochre. If you want an iridescent effect, you use a yellow underneath a green."

The Speculum and Wing Coverts

"The gadwall is the only marsh duck with a white speculum. To get that color, I use white, gesso, and a small amount of raw umber. For the wing coverts, I want a rust color. I use a mix of burnt sienna and a small amount of ultramarine blue. Burnt sienna alone is too rust-colored. For this I may well use four thin washes."

Primaries

"For the wings, I use burnt umber and a small amount of white and black. But the insides of these primaries have a greenish cast. You'll have to turn the mount a certain way to pick that up, it's so thin. So I apply two thin washes of green and black. Toward the tips it gets darker, so I use black there."

The same mix is used for the upper rump area. At the base of the tail on the rump is a greenish cast. This is a mix of Hooker's green and black.

The Legs

"The scales on the top portions of these gadwall legs I carved in with the burning pen. Then I went back with straight gesso and a real fine brush and put a little drop in each square to give the illusion of a scaly look. But first you have to gesso the legs completely, so they don't have different shades. When the scales dry, they flatten out just a little. So you have to go over them twice. But I put them on so thick, it takes a little while for them to set. So I have to be careful when I go from one side to the other that I don't bump them. But they really make a super effect. This kind of detail is a trademark of mine as I told you before, because on most flat-bottomed birds you don't see this.

Another color revealed on the gadwall's left side is rust. This is part of the wing coverts. It is a mix of burnt sienna, ultramarine blue, and dioxazine purple.

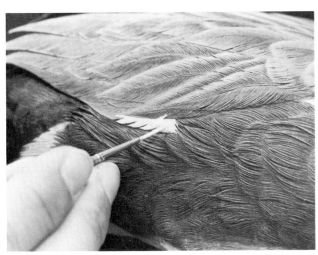

The speculum area is painted white with a small amount of raw umber.

With a small brush, Jim applies gesso on each of the crosshatched lines on the nubbins made to create a scaly effect.

Here are the speculum and another white area that is also a mix of white and raw umber.

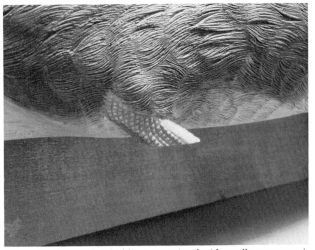

When dry, the crosshatched lines are painted with a yellow-orange mix and covered with burnt umber washes.

Shown here are the cup-shaped breast feathers that merge into vermiculation on a study mount.

Before Jim begins painting the breast feathers, he draws them on the bird with a white lead pencil, as shown on the right side. On the left he has begun painting with a small amount of gesso, white, burnt umber, and raw umber. The gesso, he says, offers better covering power.

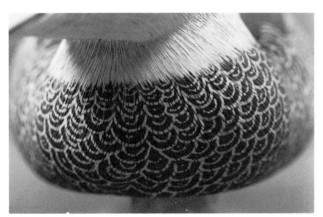

Here the breast is finished. Note the inner cups that must also be painted.

"Then I put three coats of a matte medium varnish on the legs to give them a waxy look."

Vermiculation

"Before I vermiculate, I put down a very thin wash of burnt umber. This covers up areas where the washes may have worn thin.

"I should point out that this is the only bird on which I vermiculate light over dark. This is basically because of the transition from the breast to the sides. There you'll have half-moon cup feathers going into the vermiculated pattern. So I use white on dark. The white is a mixture of gesso, titanium white, a bit of burnt umber, and raw umber. The reason I use the gesso is that it has more covering power. It'll cover anything, so when I apply gesso with regular white, I can paint the vermiculation with a single stroke.

"You can't put on just straight white. You need an amount of burnt umber that you wouldn't believe." Jim held up a spatula of white next to a study mount. The difference was apparent. "I used to put this on as straight white, then apply washes over that. But that had a way of muddying the brown I already had on.

"It's important when you're mixing any kind of color for vermiculation to make too much rather than not enough and then have to go back and try to match. It's better to mix and store.

"Vermiculation varies from one bird to another, but to most people it all looks white on a gadwall. When I'm mixing paints, then, I'll look at my mount under

The cups become vermiculated on the sides and back behind the neck. The mix used for the breast feathers is used for the vermiculation.

Results of vermiculating the area above the nubbins can be seen here.

Jim vermiculates with a No. 2 red sable brush, saying that it points up well and holds a fair amount of paint for its size.

The vermiculation continues behind the side pockets and under the tail.

On the finished bird, the extent of the vermiculating can be seen.

natural light. But when I have to rely on my overhead lights, I use a combination of cool and warm fluorescent bulbs. I think that combination works reasonably well. One way to test them is to paint the bird, put it by the window on a well-lit morning, then flip off the overhead lights. If the values of the colors don't change, obviously you're pretty close.

"I start vermiculating at the rear of the side pockets and work forward. It's easier to work and put lines down without working over what you've just painted. Also, you can get them closer together. This takes a great deal of concentration, so you don't do other things when you're vermiculating.

"It's difficult to vermiculate with white. The way the brush points up is important. You need to apply the lines so that they all have the same values. And if you go over them, you end up making the lines a little wider than you really want."

The Head

"The head I do last. The white area behind and under the bill is white and raw umber. The distinctive streaks are black and burnt umber, while the crown is burnt sienna and burnt umber. For the cape I combine black and burnt umber."

An Ideal Duck?

Through the day, the gadwall, with each successive wash, had taken on more and more of the reality of its best plumage. And the colors were as Jim had told me—subtle and beautiful.

As he put on the wavy and numerous vermiculation lines with delicate strokes of a fine brush, I asked him if there was an ideal duck for someone like me to begin with. Without looking up from the bird, he said he had started off carving a goldeneye, then went on to a broadbill, later a bufflehead, and then got into teal, the species he has been most partial to. Echoing something Larry Hayden had told me, he said, "If you keep it simple, not that any of them are really that simple, stay away from a gadwall. Try a broadbill, canvasback, bufflehead—all basically two-color birds. Starting even with a teal might be ambitious."

But as he thought more about it, he noted that "A lot of carvers start with gunning decoys. But if you want something decorative, a black duck might be a good one to start with." He added that doing the same species of duck two or three times would be advantageous. "Get something in focus. If you're working only evenings and weekends, where at best this is a part-time hobby, you'll have one bird you'll do relatively well."

Still not pausing from his painting, he continued: "If you're thinking of getting into competitions, you'll have to hone in on doing one diving duck and one puddle duck well. For example, a good diving duck is a canvasback. A good puddle or marsh duck that's not too difficult to paint is a black duck. You may be tempted to do a lot of different species, but in competitions you'll have a chance to win the ribbon or Best in Show for the best diving or puddle duck."

More on Acrylics

"What I'm learning about acrylics is that they're so relatively new, people really don't know how capable

Last to be done is the head. The feather tips are a mix of black and burnt umber. Then a series of black washes is applied to the neck, and a burnt sienna and burnt umber mix is put on the upper crown.

The results of the washes can be seen on the finished gadwall.

Jim would advise beginning carvers to try a gunning decoy. This one of a black duck, carved in 1982, has some refinement, though the body feathers are done with just a prisma color pencil. Note the bulky look to the duck and the traditional anchor in the foreground that keeps the decoy from floating away.

these paints are of holding up to light and even house dust.

"I've found that painted birds, over the course of six or eight months, will lose some of their brilliance being out in a room. My recommendation, when asked about maintaining them, is that people consider putting them under glass.

"If they're not under glass, how would I keep them clean? The best way is to dust them with a sable brush. But be careful around the primaries. And always brush with the flow of the feathers, just as I advised with steel-wooling and gessoing."

Keeping Records

"Painting didn't come easy for me. But I was fortunate to have had one of the best painters in the business helping me. He was accessible and gracious to help. That was Leo McIntosh of Woodville, New York. He worked for Ken Harris. If there was something that could help me turn corners in painting, he made it possible.

"But I just couldn't see him every day, so I made notes of what I mixed so that when I was with him, I could have things to discuss with him.

"This is something everyone should do – keep records. I'll make a whole set of notes with comments when I paint a new bird. Then I may do a whole new set of notes in later years, adding and striking things."

The Future

"People ask me when I'm going to try flat artwork. But the grass seems greener somewhere else. True, I've always been interested in the arts, in pictures and paintings. But as long as I enjoy choking on sawdust, I still have a lot of goals I want to reach with carving. I still look for some unique thing going on with these birds to make my carvings different from the next guy's. So there's still a great challenge.

"I guess, then, I really don't have to start a new field. To do that, I'd have to spend six months to a year doing nothing but get geared up for it. But, who knows, maybe somewhere down the road . . ."

6

Eye Sizes, Patterns, and Painting Notes

> The patterns in this book are half-size. To make a full-size working pattern, you must enlarge the drawing to the following scale.
>
> Scale: 1″ on this pattern equals 2″ on full-size pattern.

MARSH DUCKS

Species	Sex	Eye Color	Eye Size
black duck	drake	brown	11 mm
baikal teal	drake	dark brown	10 mm
blue-winged teal	drake and hen	brown	9 mm
cinnamon teal	drake	red-orange	9 mm
cinnamon teal	hen	brown	9 mm
gadwall	drake	brown	11 mm
green-winged teal	drake and hen	hazel	9 mm
pintail	drake and hen	brown	11 mm
shoveler	drake	yellow	10 mm
shoveler	hen	brown	10 mm
wood duck	drake	dark red	12 mm

BLACK DUCK DRAKE   1984

Undercoat	Two to three thin coats of Deft; two thin washes of gesso, raw umber, and small amount of yellow ochre; then airbrush until cover is even.
Head	Brush on titanium white, raw umber, and small amount of yellow ochre; crown and ultramarine blue and burnt sienna; then raw sienna; wash with burnt umber.
Base coat for body	Four to five washes of burnt sienna, ultramarine blue, and small amount of burnt umber; then airbrush until desired shade reached; with Langnickel #617 No. 2 brush, put feather tips on with a mix of burnt sienna, burnt umber, white, and yellow ochre; then brush on straight burnt umber on feather tips; darker on top of back; sides, breast, and rump area from base out a mix of darker base mix; then greenish cast in tail area (Hooker's green and black). At this point, put greenish cast on small feathers if any showing on wings (raw umber, Hooker's green, and small amount of black); put ivory black on tips and quills; ivory black quills on all applicable feathers; a dark base coat on all feather splits.
Tertials	Lower part dark brown (ultramarine blue and burnt sienna); then next two feathers a mix of dioxazine purple and black (airbrush); smoke feathers are white, small amounts of burnt umber and black; brush on a light spray of burnt umber; quills a straight burnt umber; matte medium varnish on all quills.
Speculum	Gesso, thalo blue or ultramarine blue and dioxazine purple with bronzing powder (Venus blue); top part of each section alizarin red and reddish bronzing powder; next a couple of washes of black; then thalo green watered in on last section (bottom) of speculum; ivory black on tips; then thin white tips a mix of white and raw umber.
Bill	Gesso first for even acceptance of paint; use yellow ochre, cadmium yellow, raw umber, and small amount of black; black nail, and under bill is a brownish black.
Wings	Basic color same as base coat of bird; ivory black from tips back, quills a burnt umber; greenish cast is Hooker's green; cream tips area white and burnt umber.
Legs and feet	Gesso; gesso scales are Hansa orange, alizarin red and burnt umber; if too dark, lighten with yellow ochre; nails ivory black; webs underneath darker; airbrush with burnt umber and black.
Under tail and wings	White, small amount of black and burnt umber; straight white on tips of feathers and quills; then washes of black and burnt umber.

Jim's 1984 black duck is a fine example of his search for new poses.

Here can be seen the crossing of the primary feathers under the tertials and also how far the leg extends from the body.

Study the very distinct black streaks in the face in this photo. These are a mix of yellow ochre, white, and raw umber.

This is a good detail of the webbed foot, which was painted with a mix of red, Hansa orange, and burnt umber.

The groupings of tertial and scapular feathers can be seen here.

Jim used straight white on the edges of these tail feathers.

Black Duck Drake
1983

Black Duck Drake
1983

2 ¼" Thick

Scale: 1" on this pattern equals 2" on full-size pattern.

BAIKAL TEAL DRAKE 1983

Undercoat Two coats of gesso and raw umber; white and raw umber for lower sides and under tail; for vermiculated areas on sides and behind head put coats of white, Grumbacher gray and raw umber.

Breast Dark shade first of white, burnt sienna, small amount of raw sienna, burnt umber, and black; center of breast light – add white; black spots a Mars black; then feather tips are white and a small amount of raw umber; brush used for spots a Langnickel #5180 No. 1; washes of burnt umber and burnt sienna; matte medium varnish for a waxy look.

Head Cream color area first – unbleached titanium white, burnt umber, and small amount of raw sienna; green area second – Hooker's green, thalo green, and small amount of black;' then flick on yellow ochre and cadmium yellow for feather tips; then washes of green mix, thalo blue, and black; black area third – ultramarine blue, burnt sienna, and small amount of black; flick on for feather tips white and raw umber; then washes of burnt umber on tips.

Bill Black, ultramarine blue, and burnt sienna.

Back Wash entire area with a mix of yellow ochre, raw umber, and small amounts of black and burnt umber for a gold cast; flick white on all applicable feather tips including tail area, darker from the base out. Apply all black areas on tertials, streamers and quills – ultramarine blue and burnt sienna; put gesso on light area of streamers; then washes of white, yellow ochre, and burnt umber; darken this mix and water in from base out; for the rust area, use raw sienna, a small amount of burnt sienna, and burnt umber; apply black and raw umber washes over entire area; put white bars on next – white and raw umber.

Under tail Rust area first – burnt sienna, small amount of raw sienna and burnt umber; then black area – ultramarine blue and burnt sienna; next, white feather tips; then washes of burnt umber and black.

Speculum Gesso, yellow ochre; thalo green, black, and bronzing powder.

Vermiculation #00 Rapidograph pen; then spray with Krylon Matte Spray #1311.

Legs and Feet Yellow ochre, white, and burnt umber; wash with burnt umber; then matte medium varnish.

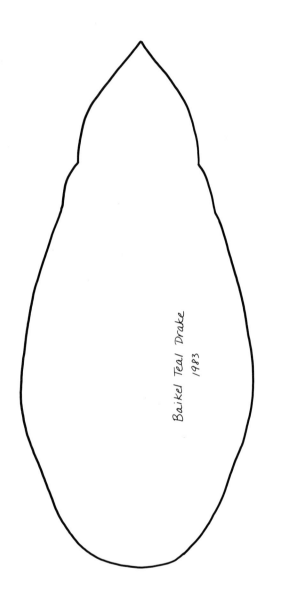

Baikel Teal Drake
1983

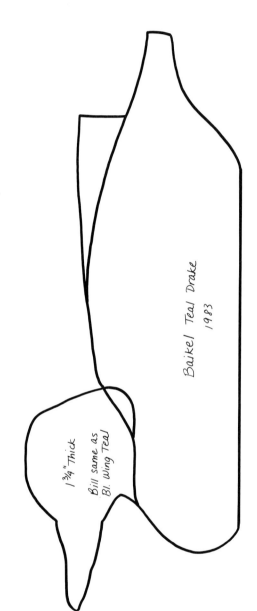

Baikel Teal Drake
1983

1¾" Thick

Bill same as
Bl. Wing Teal

Scale: 1" on this pattern equals 2" on full-size pattern.

BLUE-WINGED TEAL DRAKE   1980

Breast, sides, and under rump	Mix white base, small amounts of Grumbacher red and burnt sienna; if too pinkish, add a small amount of burnt umber and raw sienna or even black; for breast, back, and one-third of sides, blend in a wash of raw sienna; flick on above mix to breast and blend into one-third of sides and under rump.
Head	Mix white into black base, add small amounts of burnt umber and thalo blue, two or three thin coats; black crown is ultramarine blue, burnt sienna, and small amount of black; white feather tips; white half-moon is white, Grumbacher gray, thalo violet and thalo green watered in; then washes of burnt umber and black; bill is black.
Spots on breast and sides	Use same mix used for base coat for back and upper part of tail area (raw umber, burnt umber, and small amount of black); then washes of burnt umber and black for desired shade.
Long feathers on back	Darker on outside half (thalo green and black); centers a mix of white, yellow ochre, and burnt umber; quills raw sienna; apply washes of burnt umber to get desired shade.
Blue feathers	Ultramarine blue with white and burnt umber; then flick on white feather tips; finally, one thin wash of burnt umber.

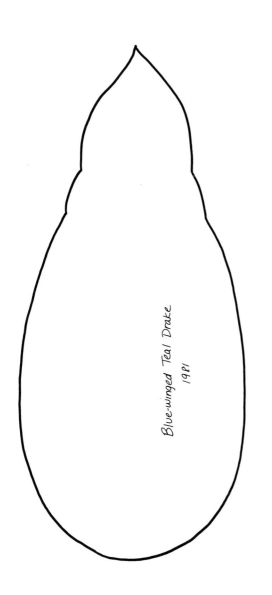

Blue-winged Teal Drake
1981

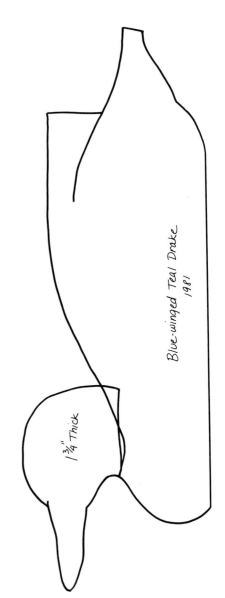

Blue-winged Teal Drake
1981

1¾" Thick

Scale: 1" on this pattern equals 2" on full-size pattern.

BLUE-WINGED TEAL HEN AND CINNAMON TEAL HEN   1983

Undercoat	Deft sealer and gesso; gesso and raw umber on head and lower sides (behind bill area is whiter).
Back, breast, and top part of sides	Paint this area raw umber, burnt umber, and small amount of black (lighter on sides, darker on back area); breast darker than sides; sides burnt umber and small amount of black; flick white on all feather tips (white and raw umber); darken from base out with raw umber and black; feathers next to speculum have a greenish cast—Hooker's green and black.
Speculum	Gesso, then cadmium yellow; wet center before applying Hooker's green, and black; then a wash of black.
Blue side area	Ultramarine blue, white, and burnt umber; white feather tips; wash of light burnt umber.
Legs	Yellow-orange cast—yellow ochre, white, burnt sienna, and burnt umber.
Bill	Yellow cast first of yellow ochre, white, and burnt umber; top two-thirds a mix of black, white, and burnt umber for dusk color; wet and put on spots of a dusky color.
Head	White and raw umber at base of bill and under chin; darken crown and eye area; streaks on crown are raw umber, burnt umber, and small amount of black; also streaks of yellow ochre and white; thin washes of black and burnt umber.
Wings	Greenish cast on inside half; quills raw sienna.

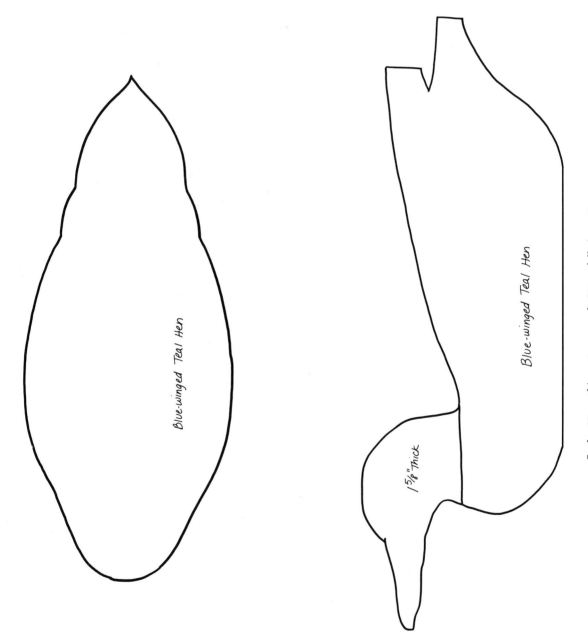

Blue-winged Teal Hen

Blue-winged Teal Hen

1⅝" Thick

Scale: 1" on this pattern equals 2" on full-size pattern.

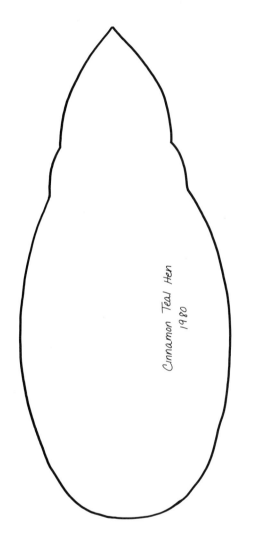

Cinnamon Teal Hen
1980

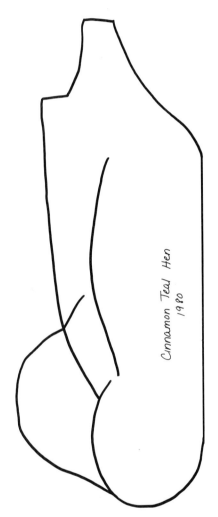

Cinnamon Teal Hen
1980

Scale: 1" on this pattern equals 2" on full-size pattern.

CINNAMON TEAL DRAKE   1982

Undercoat	Gesso and small amount of yellow ochre.
Sides, breast, head, and under rump	Thin coats of burnt sienna and ultramarine blue in 4-to-1 ratio; can always lighten with yellow ochre; yellow ochre on all feather tips, darken from base out on sides with burnt umber; crown of head and undertail is black (burnt sienna and ultramarine blue).
Tail and wings	Raw umber, burnt umber, and small amount of black; wings have greenish cast (thalo green and black).
Back and top of tail area	Put on white feather tips (white and raw umber); darker from base out (raw umber and black); put in reddish vermiculation with white mix, then washes of side mix; feather splits with ink pen.
Long feathers on back	Centers a mix of yellow ochre, raw sienna, burnt umber, and white; lower half of tertials a greenish cast; use thalo green and small amount of black; after blending centers, put raw sienna from base out on quills; quills of tertial feathers yellow ochre and small amount of white in centers.
Blue feathers on sides	Ultramarine blue, white, and burnt umber.
First feathers behind blue feathers	Ultramarine blue, white, and small amount of burnt umber; then mix in a small amount of Hooker's green.
Legs	Yellow ochre and white; can mix in a small amount of burnt umber; then a wash of burnt umber.
Speculum	Gesso, yellow, thalo green, black, and bronzing powder; then a wash of black.

Shown here is a cinnamon teal that won First Place in Species at the 1984 World Championship Wildfowl Carving Competition. The blue portion of the upper wing coverts contrasts to the cinnamon color of the breast and sides.

Here can be studied the feather layout for the side pockets, the breast, and how the primaries come off the body.

Notice how Jim turned the head to the left and slightly upward. Study the bill details.

Notice the feather detailing and flow lines on the head here.

Another photo of the same cinnamon teal details the stoning lines and feather splits.

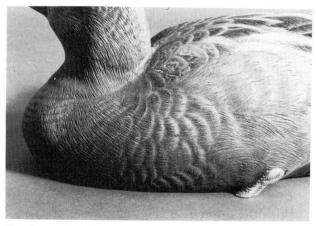

Note the transition of the feathers from the head to the breast to the side pocket on the right side.

This resting cinnamon teal drake won First Place in Species at the 1983 World Championships, and is owned by H. P. Andrews of Jackson, Michigan.

To be studied here are the feathers on the rump as well as the tertials. The light centers are a mix of yellow ochre, raw sienna, burnt umber, and white.

A view of the rear of the bird shows good rump details and primaries below those on the cinnamon teal previously photographed.

A good detail of the head shows the bill buried in the wing. Note the feather splits of the feathers over the bill.

See how the side pockets meet the speculum and tertial areas.

A rear view shows how the primaries are located when the duck is resting.

This is the right side, now finished, of the cinnamon teal drake photographed in different stages throughout this book.

This photo offers good rear view details.

The same bird seen from above shows the layout of all back feathers.

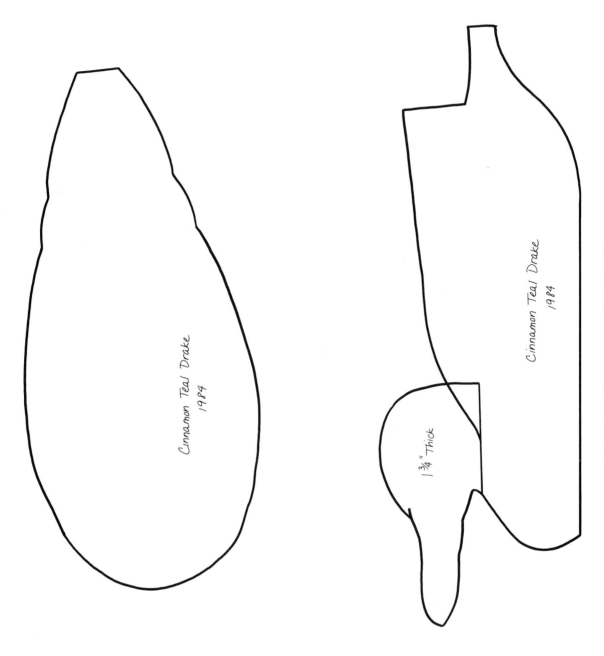

Cinnamon Teal Drake
1984

Cinnamon Teal Drake
1984

1¾" Thick

Scale: 1" on this pattern equals 2" on full-size pattern.

GADWALL DRAKE 1984

Undercoat	Deft; gesso.
Lower sides, under rump and head	Washes of titanium white, gesso, and a small amount of raw umber.
Sides, breast, and back of neck	Ultramarine blue and burnt sienna mixed; breast is a darker shade of black; water in on back.
Long back feathers	White base, small amounts of burnt umber and black—long back feathers watered into short feathers (can also put this shade on tail top and bottom and under wings); add black and burnt umber for area next to shorter feathers; airbrush tips with white and small amount of raw umber; watery wash of raw sienna for quills; put burnt umber wash on area after shorter feathers are completed.
Short back feathers	Raw sienna base, small amounts of white, burnt umber, burnt sienna—blend into back area; centers of feathers are a mix of burnt umber and small amount of white; quills are straight burnt umber; flick white and raw umber on tips; raw sienna on same feather tips; then washes of burnt umber over all feathers.
Wings	Burnt umber, small amounts of white and black, black on tips; inside half has greenish cast (Hooker's green and black); quills a watery raw sienna—wash of burnt umber; no white on feather tips.
Rump and tail area	Black area—ultramarine blue, burnt sienna, and small amount of black; greenish cast at base of tail (Hooker's green and black); white on feather tips, then washes of black and burnt umber.
Speculum	White, gesso, and small amount of raw umber.
Three Colors on Sides:	
Rust	Burnt sienna, ultramarine blue, and dioxazine purple.
Black	Burnt sienna and ultramarine blue; white on all feather tips.
White	White and raw umber.
Vermiculation	White, small amount of gesso, burnt umber, and raw umber; then a thin wash of burnt umber.
Head	White and raw umber for white area behind and under bill; streaks are black and burnt umber; crown is burnt sienna and burnt umber; cape is black and burnt umber; then washes of burnt umber.
Bill	Lower part a mix of burnt sienna, raw sienna, and yellow ochre watered in; top a mix of ultramarine blue and burnt sienna; airbrush into orange area.
Feet and legs	Yellow-orange mix with burnt umber washes.

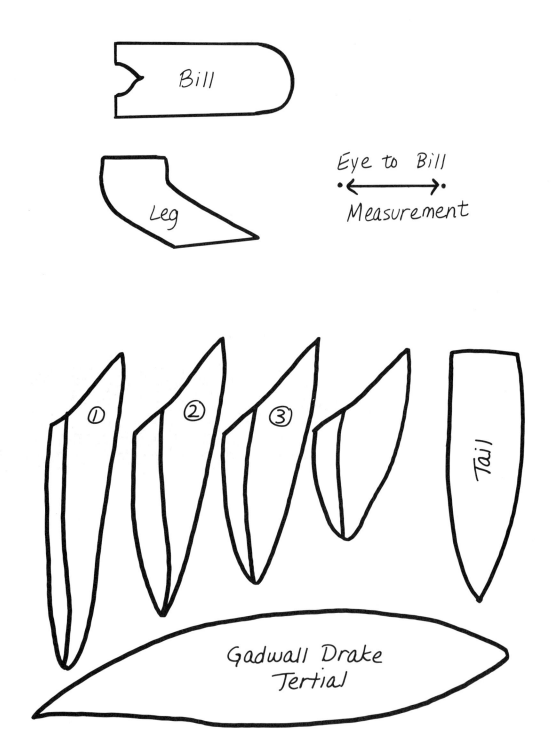

Bill

Leg

Eye to Bill
Measurement

① ② ③

Tail

Gadwall Drake
Tertial

Scale: 1″ on this pattern equals 2″ on full-size pattern.

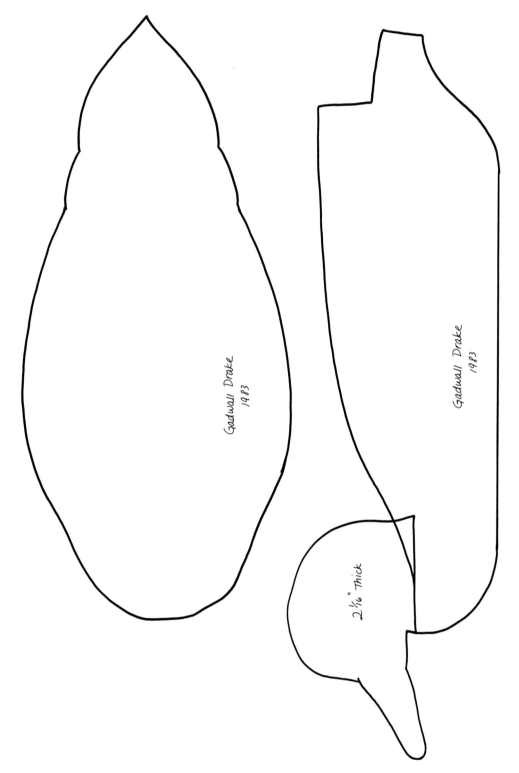

Gadwall Drake
1983

Gadwall Drake
1983

2 ⁷⁄₁₆" Thick

Scale: 1" on this pattern equals 2" on full-size pattern.

GREEN-WINGED TEAL DRAKE   1983

Sides, rump, and front part of back	Gray area—use white, Grumbacher gray, and small amount of raw umber.
Breast	Thin washes of white, raw sienna, burnt sienna, and burnt umber; black spots are black and burnt umber (same as vermiculation); put on straight white feather tips; then washes of burnt umber; darker close to neck; matte medium varnish on breast for a waxy look.
Head	Gesso; two to three thin coats of burnt sienna, small amount of burnt umber, and yellow ochre on brown area; green area is Hooker's green and black; then flick on yellow ochre and cadmium yellow; for bluish area use thalo blue and black; then washes of green mix and thalo blue and black; crown is darker—use burnt umber and burnt sienna; do white feather tips; yellow ochre feather tips on face; for cream line use white, yellow ochre, and burnt umber.
Bill	Gesso; for leathery look, use burnt sienna and ultramarine blue; brownish cast on lower part of bill, darker on top.
Long back feathers, top of tail area, and tail	Raw umber, small amounts of white, black, and burnt umber; then water in center area with a mix of burnt umber, raw umber, an a small amount of black; quills darker; white and raw umber on feather edges, including the tail; then washes of raw umber.
Speculum	Gesso, cadmium yellow; Hooker's green and black washes; white edges.
Under rump	Paint champagne-color area a mix of yellow ochre, white (light); cup (round out the tip of) brush and put on raw sienna tips; white at very tip of tail; then wash of burnt umber.
Vermiculation	Black and burnt umber; put a wash of Grumbacher gray on sides and back.
Legs	White, Grumbacher gray, and small amount of cobalt blue; webs darker; raw umber wash; matte medium finish.

Do not forget white sidebars.

This green-winged teal drake, carved in 1979, took First Place in Species at the Midwest Decoy Contest held in Monroe, Michigan.

The vermiculation is a mix of black and burnt umber. The distinctive green area on the sides of the head is a mix of Hooker's green and black.

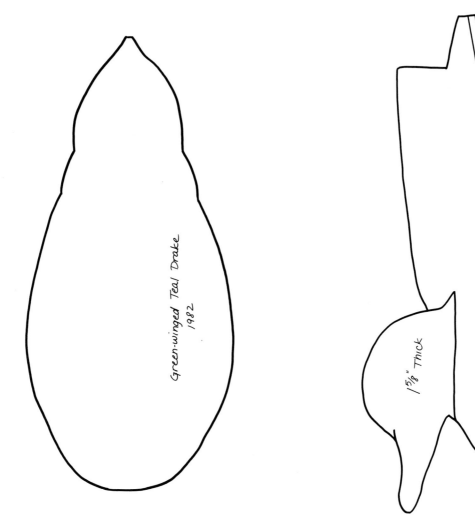

Green-winged Teal Drake
1982

Green-winged Teal Drake
1982

5/8" Thick

Scale: 1" on this pattern equals 2" on full-size pattern.

GREEN-WINGED TEAL HEN   1976

Undercoat	Gesso lower part of breast, sides, and under rump; apply thin gesso on top.
Back, upper sides, and breast	Use a mix of burnt umber, raw umber, ultramarine blue; apply as thin coats (not too dark); white flecks are white, burnt umber, raw umber and small amount of black from base out; thin washes of raw umber; raw sienna on feather tips.
Head	Mix of raw umber and gesso for base coat; streaks are a mix of burnt umber, raw umber, and ultramarine blue; then streaks of raw sienna and thin white; apply washes of burnt umber; leave whiter at base of bill and under chin.
Bill	Thalo violet with small amount of black; but first gesso whole bill; then purple mix into water; black (ultramarine blue and burnt sienna) watered into purple; coat with matte medium varnish.
Speculum	Paint area with gesso, then a coat of cadmium yellow; wet center and use Hooker's green and black on lower area with white tips; raw sienna on other end of speculum.

Revision 1978
Back

Burnt umber, raw umber, and ultramarine blue from base out; split feathers done with #1 Rapidograph pen; if overall body is too dark, wash with burnt umber and raw sienna.

Revision 1979
Bill

Paint bill with gesso; then for entire bill apply a couple of thin coats of Payne's gray and white for blue gray, then black on top ridge of bill; next, Payne's gray, white, and small amount of black; purple watered in on lower corner; last, Grumbacher purple and thalo violet mix; don't forget black spots.

Gold area on feathers

Put white on when putting on feather tips; put raw sienna on, then washes of raw umber and burnt umber.

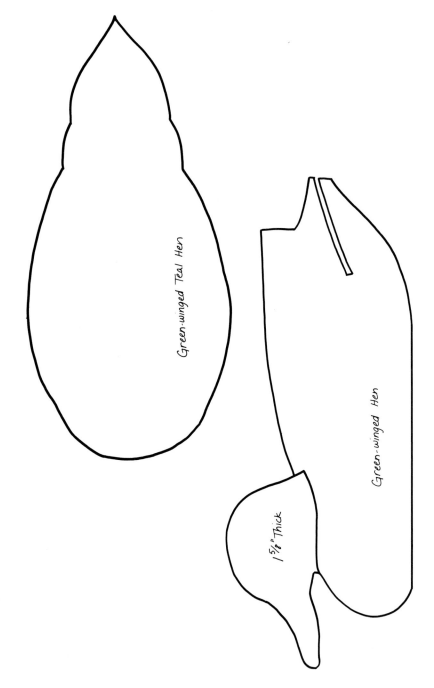

Green-winged Teal Hen

Green-winged Hen

1⅝" Thick

Scale: 1" on this pattern equals 2" on full-size pattern.

PINTAIL DRAKE 1984

First lay out horns on head with pencil; then paint as follows.

Breast, sides, rump, and front part of back	Grayish brown area—white, small amount of Payne's gray and raw umber for warmth; then one straight white wash on breast only; white feather tips on lower sides and under rump area; on breast, watery burnt umber feather tips; then straight white washes; matte medium varnish on breast for waxy look.
Head	Equal parts of burnt umber and raw umber, and small amount of white for brown shade; then light washes over entire brown area (not too dark); put in white horns, then blend white hairs into darker area, then dark brown hairs; green area in front of horns is thalo green and bronzing powder; thalo violet, small amount of black and bronzing powder; nape of neck ultramarine blue and burnt sienna; small feathers on crown are white, raw umber and small amount of raw sienna; then flick burnt umber-raw sienna mix, then one wash of same; straight burnt umber feather flecks on cheek.
Bill	Gesso, white, small amount thalo blue and Grumbacher gray; can darken with burnt umber; paint entire bill, then mix ultramarine blue and burnt sienna watered into bluish gray color.
Long feathers on back	Use the first mix on upper rump area (white with small amount Grumbacher gray and raw umber); white and small amount of raw umber only on lower half of streamer feathers; black centers a mix of Mars black and burnt umber; Mars black on quills; white and raw umber on tips (thin line); one wash of raw umber.
Legs	White, small amount of ultramarine blue and black; one wash of black.
Under tail area	White area first (next to tail feathers), white and raw umber; then black area, top and under tail is ultramarine blue, burnt sienna, and small amount of Mars black; put champagne color on next—white and yellow ochre; then light raw sienna for tips; then light burnt umber wash.
Wings	Burnt umber and small amounts white and black; white and raw umber mix on feather tips; black and brown quills; then one wash of black.
Vermiculation	Three parts black to one part burnt umber mix; black splits; one burnt umber wash; burnt umber on low areas; airbrush straight white on area where breast and side vermiculation meet.

This 1984 pintail drake carving shows the duck's bellowed-out chest.

Here the head details of the duck can be studied.

This photo shows the stoning lines on the breast as well as a prominent throat muscle.

Note the drooping tertials of the pintail and the low-set primaries.

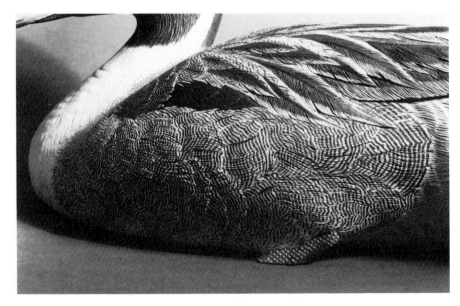

The side pocket groupings are still noticeable under the heavy vermiculation. For this Jim will use a 3-to-1 mix of black and burnt umber.

The top view reveals the dark centers of the scapulars. These are a mix of Mars black and burnt umber.

Study the rump area of this pintail.

The six-inch tail of the pintail, curving to one side, is detachable to make transporting the bird easier.

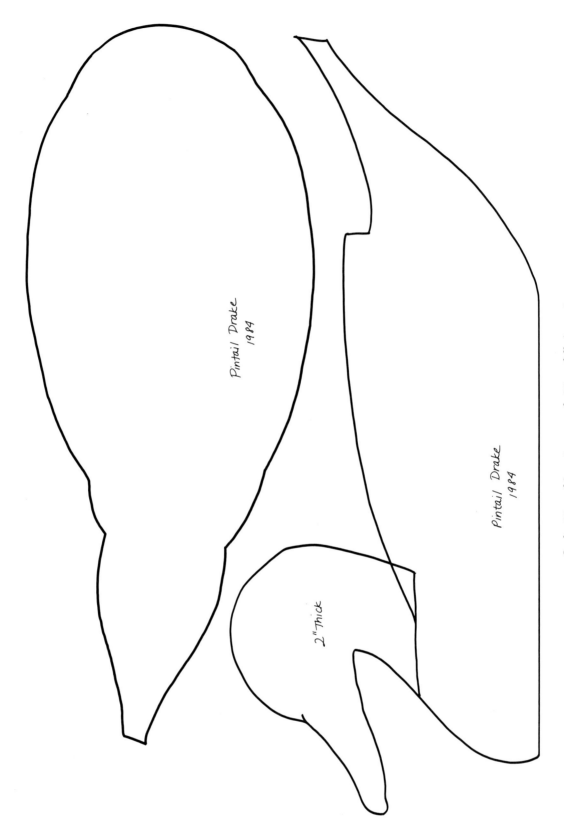

Pintail Drake
1984

Pintail Drake
1984

2" Thick

Scale: 1" on this pattern equals 2" on full-size pattern.

PINTAIL HEN   1979

Undercoat	Deft, then thin coat of gesso.
Head, lower sides, and under rump	·Thin coats of gesso, burnt umber, and small amount of raw sienna.
Back, upper sides, breast, and under tail	Thin washes of burnt umber, raw umber, and small amount of black; flick white on all feather tips; dark from base out (burnt umber, raw umber and small amount of black); feather splits done with ink pen; washes of raw umber and burnt umber; white flecks for gold area of feathers, then raw sienna; quills are dark, almost black; breast has more raw sienna cast; crown has a couple of thin washes of raw sienna and burnt umber; then put on all dark feather flecks (burnt umber, raw umber, and small amount of black); apply some raw sienna flecks; then washes of burnt umber and raw sienna.
Bill	Paint entire bill a color of slate blue (white, thalo blue mixed); then darken with Grumbacher gray; hen has darker area, same as drake pintail, on lower corners and top of bill – this could be done with slate color that is almost black.
Wings	Definite white feather tips with raw sienna quills.

Pintail Hen
1981

Pintail Hen
1981

1 7/8" Thick

Scale: 1" on this pattern equals 2" on full-size pattern.

SHOVELER DRAKE   1983

Undercoat	Thin gesso—two coats of Deft brand.
Sides	2nd step, apply white and small black mix on lower and rear corner.
	3rd step, to one-third top area apply yellow ochre and white mix (more white than yellow); add small amount of burnt umber (may need a wash of it).
Rump	4th step, apply a mix of Liquitex burnt sienna, ultramarine blue, burnt umber, and a small amount of yellow ochre; water this into blue area.
Breast	Paint area with white and Grumbacher gray; follow with straight white feather tips; use washes of white for desired shade.
Head	Put a thin wash of gesso and a thin wash of yellow ochre over entire head; start with thin coats of two parts of thalo green, one part of Hooker's green, one part of black over entire head; for highlights, put yellow ochre on first, then thalo blue wash over entire head; crown is black and under chin is black (burnt sienna and ultramarine blue); put all white feather tips on crown of head now (white mixed with raw umber); put brown umber on crown and under chin; thalo blue and black on bluish area; wash of thalo blue and one wash of black over entire head.
Bill	Paint lower mandible with a mix of white, cadmium red, and small amount of black (ultramarine blue and burnt sienna).
Back	Paint area raw umber and black; then paint tertial area darker; tertial feathers have a greenish cast on lower half—use thalo green and black; put washes of raw umber on white feather tips; splits done with ink pen; quills are darker; quills straight white on tertials.
Blue on sides	Apply gesso first, then ultramarine blue and white; then add burnt umber; apply straight ultramarine blue on upper part (watered into lighter blue area).
Speculum	Gesso first, then paint whole area with cadmium yellow; mix or blend in thalo green and Hooker's green and black and bronzing powder; then apply wash of straight black; white on edges.
Tail	Paint entire tail area white and burnt umber and a small amount of black; for darker areas, add black; spots are blended in with this darker mix; straight white goes on feather tips; then apply wash of burnt umber.
Wings	Apply burnt umber, white and small amount of black; feather tips are darker, so add more black to the mix; greenish cast is gotten with thalo green and black; quills are darker (more black to original mix); then apply burnt umber washes; white on feather tips (white and burnt umber).
Vermiculation	Ink pen used on sides; matte #1311 sprayed on sides; then a wash of burnt umber.
Feet	Hansa orange, white, cadmium yellow mix; then apply a wash of burnt umber.

Jim carves his shoveler drakes with their heads thrust forward because these birds are usually sifting water.

Note the details on the head and bill. The bill creases were done with a No. 9 pencil, and the lamellae were done with a burning tool.

On the first row of feathers on the base of the tail is a greenish cast. This is achieved with a mix of thalo green and black.

Note the layout of side pocket feathers. Jim will use an ink pen for the vermiculation, then spray it with #1311 Krylon matte spray.

Here the transition from breast to side pockets to back is well shown.

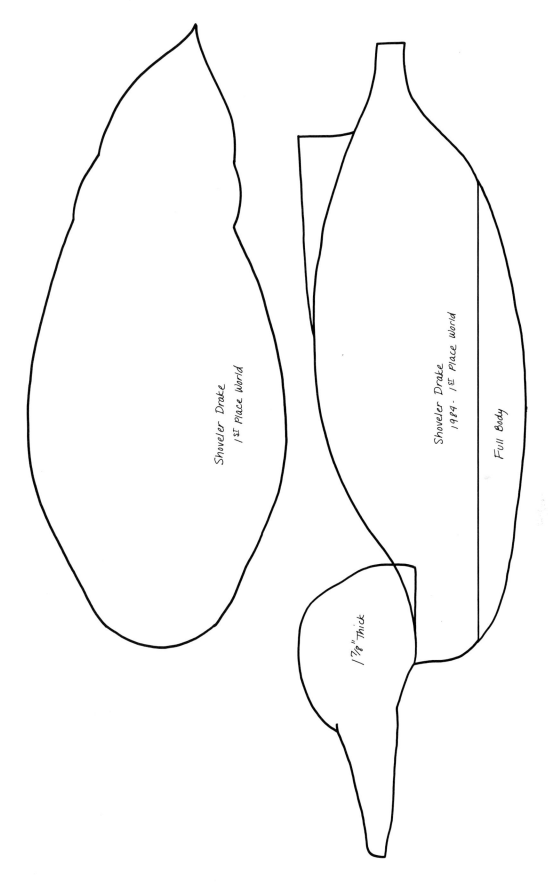

Shoveler Drake
1ST Place World

Shoveler Drake
1984 - 1ST Place World

Full Body

1 7/8" Thick

Scale: 1" on this pattern equals 2" on full-size pattern.

SHOVELER HEN   1983

Undercoat	Deft, gesso and small amount of raw umber; head and lower sides a mix of gesso, raw umber and burnt umber.
Back, sides, and breast	Paint thin coats of burnt umber, raw umber and small amounts of black; lighter on sides and darker on breasts; sides should be burnt umber and small amounts of black; fleck white on all feather tips (white and raw umber shaded with small amount of raw sienna); darken from base of feathers out with burnt umber, raw umber and black; put greenish cast on lower half of tertials and airbrush inner sides of tertials. Apply two to three washes of burnt umber, one to two washes of raw sienna, and a wash of thin, straight black; sides have more of a raw sienna cast.
Speculum	Gesso, cadmium yellow, thalo green, Hooker's green, and bronzing powder; wash of straight black; white on edges.
Blue on sides	Gesso, ultramarine blue, white, and small amount of burnt umber; straight white for feather tips and one thin wash of burnt umber.
Head	Water in white area behind bill and under chin (white and raw umber); burnt umber, raw umber, and black for crown and streaks; raw sienna flecks on face; crown lines a gold color; put on feather lines with white (white, raw umber, and small amount of raw sienna); then go over entire head with one thin wash of straight watery raw sienna.
Bill	Gesso, sand; first a mix of Hansa orange, cadmium yellow, and white; darken with raw umber; top part raw umber, yellow ochre, and Hooker's green; raw umber on top; spots green; nail brownish black.
Feet	Hansa orange, white, and cadmium yellow; thin wash of burnt umber; matte medium varnish (same as on shoveler drake).

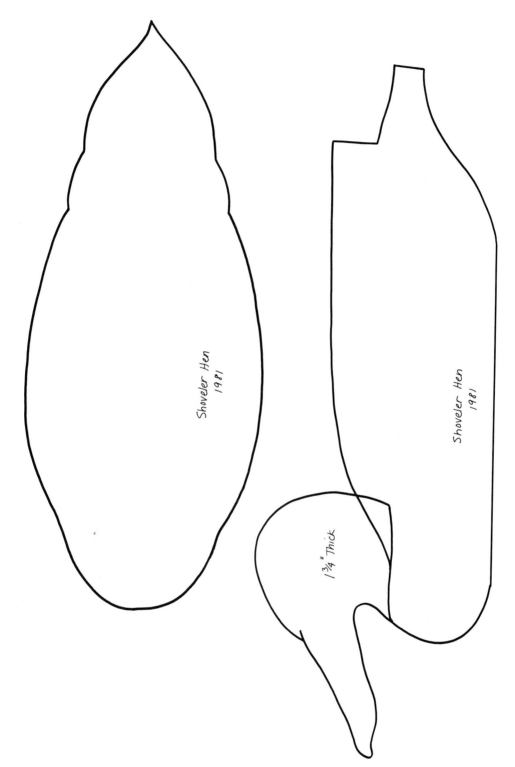

Shoveler Hen
1981

Shoveler Hen
1981

1¾" Thick

Scale: 1" on this pattern equals 2" on full-size pattern.

WOOD DUCK DRAKE   1978

1st step

Paint lower breast, sides, and under rump a mix of white and Payne's gray for an off-shade of white.

2nd step

For sides, a mix of yellow ochre, small amount of raw sienna, and white; tone it down with burnt umber; then thin washes of burnt umber; vermiculate with black brush or pen.

3rd step

For breast, paint black, flick on feather tips (heavy); washes of burnt sienna and dioxazine purple; small burnt umber mix, with diamonds.

4th step

For head, put in white area first (white and raw umber); put on all green areas next (Hooker's green and black); crown washes of Hooker's green over cadmium yellow, then thalo blue over area; lower cheek is thalo violet over thalo blue.

5th step

For bill, first white, gesso and small amount of raw umber over entire bill (three coats); then yellow (cadmium yellow, yellow ochre and small amount of white); red is Grumbacher red and small amount of black; black is ultramarine blue and burnt sienna.

6th step

For back, tail, and under rump, fleck white on all feather tips; then washes of raw umber on center of back; thalo blue and thalo violet on sides; Hooker's green on center back feathers; tail area a Hooker's green and black mix. (Revision 1983 – for back, first burnt umber, raw umber, and small amount of black – much darker on tail area; white feather tips; apply a black mix under tail.)

7th step

Vermiculation (pen or brush).

8th step

Long hairs on side – burnt umber and black mix, with streaks of yellow ochre and raw sienna.

9th step

Purple area – dioxazine purple, burnt sienna, and ultramarine blue.

10th step

Wings – paint entire wing a mix of burnt umber, raw umber, and a small amount of black; flick white on all feather tips; thalo silver on outside edges with thalo blue and thalo violet over inside; black washes over same.

11th step

Speculum – mix Hooker's green and thalo blue and wash over streaked area.

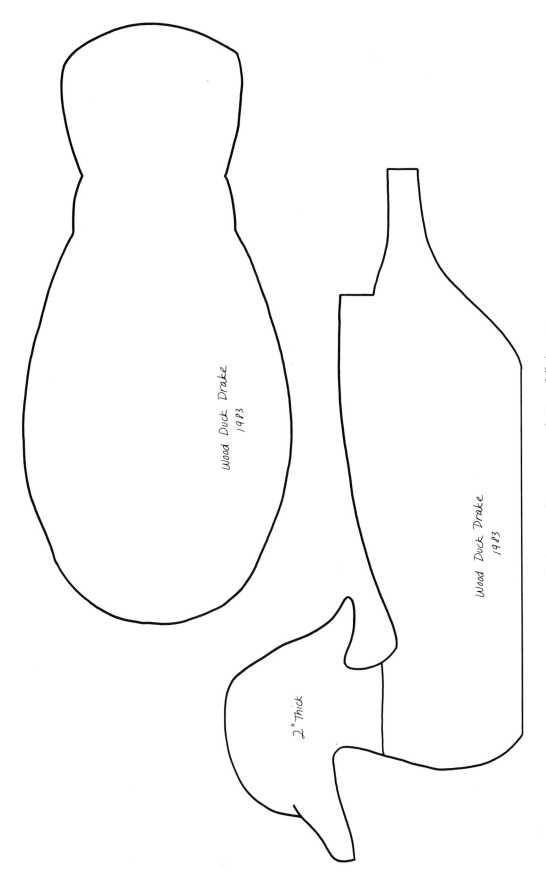

Wood Duck Drake
1983

Wood Duck Drake
1983

2" Thick

Scale: 1" on this pattern equals 2" on full-size pattern.

DIVING DUCKS

Species	Sex	Eye Color	Eye Size
bufflehead	drake	brown	10 mm
canvasback	drake	red	11 mm
canvasback	hen	brown	11 mm
harlequin	drake	brown	10 mm
hooded merganser	drake	yellow	10 mm
hooded merganser	hen	hazel	10 mm
redhead	drake	straw yellow	11 mm
redhead	hen	brown	11 mm
ring-necked duck	drake	straw yellow	10 mm
ring-necked duck	hen	brown	10 mm
ruddy	drake	brown	10 mm

BUFFLEHEAD DRAKE   1982

Undercoat	Gesso.
Breast, sides, under rump, and upper sides of back	First a mix of white, Grumbacher gray, and small amount of raw umber; straight white on feather tips, but with a yellow ochre cast – can use a wash of yellow ochre or washes of straight white and matte medium varnish mixed.
Head	For white area, try straight white first, then a wash of darker shade; for green area, thalo green and black; for purple area, Grumbacher purple or violet and ultramarine blue; then bronzing powders on green and purple areas.
Back	Brownish black is burnt sienna and ultramarine blue; then into white of neck and breast; straight black on feather tips; quills are black; then washes of black.
Tail	White, small amounts of black and burnt umber over entire tail; off-white feather tips are white and raw umber; quills darker; then washes of black or burnt umber.
Bill	Paint entire bill Grumbacher gray, white, and small amount of raw umber; then airbrush lower sides and tip a lighter shade; black nail.
Feet	Grumbacher red, white and burnt umber.

Jim has this bufflehead drake's head in an alerted position.

Here can be studied the shape of the bill as well as head details.

Here is the feather pattern for the right side pocket. Note the feather splits and leg nubbin.

This offers a good view of the top of the bufflehead. Note the position of the head.

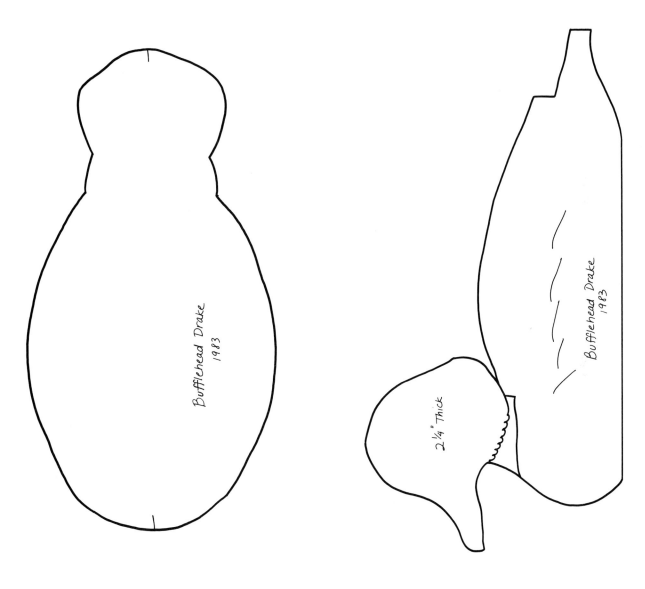

Bufflehead Drake
1983

Bufflehead Drake
1983

2¼" Thick

Scale: 1" on this pattern equals 2" on full-size pattern.

CANVASBACK DRAKE   1983

Undercoat   Deft, then gesso full strength.

Sides, top, under rump   Thin coats of white and small amounts of raw umber; after vermiculating, apply matte medium spray; then washes of white and small amount of raw umber; then one wash of Payne's gray; feather tips area a watery raw umber.

Breast and tail area   First use ultramarine blue and burnt sienna for the black; then white flecks of white and raw umber on all feather tips of these two areas; then washes of straight black and burnt umber; tail area more brownish.

Head   Gesso head feathers into black breast; then thin washes of burnt sienna and burnt umber over entire head; black (ultramarine blue and burnt sienna) on crown and cheeks next to bill and under bill; black feather tips on cheek; white feather tips on crown, then thin washes of black; Grumbacher red for highlights on cheeks.

Bill   Gesso first; black is ultramarine blue and burnt sienna; under bill is burnt umber.

Vermiculation   #00 Rapidograph pen; white and raw umber from base out on all feathers first, then one thin wash of Payne's gray; washes of white and small amount of raw umber; one wash of Grumbacher gray.

Speculum   Thalo silver, small amount of black, and burnt umber; white on tips; black edge is burnt sienna and ultramarine blue; then one wash of Grumbacher gray.

The canvasback drake, a bird featured in various stages throughout this book, can be studied here. The heavy vermiculation on the tertial feathers was done with a Rapidograph pen and indelible ink.

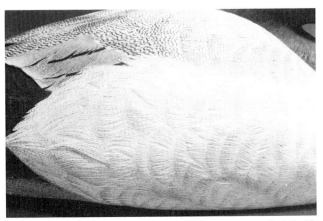

Here the layout of feathers and their splits can be seen on the left side pocket. Note the speculum in the upper left corner.

Note here the details of the rump and tail, and the position of the crossed primaries.

Notice the stoning grooves and the distinctive shape of the canvasback's bill.

This photo allows you to study the back of the bird.

Canvasback Drake
1984

2³⁄₈" Thick

Canvasback Drake
1984

2³⁄₈" Thick

Scale: 1" on this pattern equals 2" on full-size pattern.

CANVASBACK HEN   1984

Undercoat	Deft and full-strength gesso.
Sides, top, and under rump	White, small amount of raw umber.
Breast and upper tail area	Dark mix of raw umber, burnt umber, and small amounts of yellow ochre and white; white feather tips are white and small amounts of yellow ochre and raw umber; put raw sienna on breast feathers only; put on individually, leaving lower breast feathers with white tips; for tail area, darker from base out; then darken splits; then washes of burnt umber.
Head	Put light cream color around eyes and under chin – white and small amounts of raw umber and yellow ochre; dark area is burnt umber, white, small amount of yellow ochre and burnt sienna (can darken with mix left over from breast area); crown is darker; white feather tips; behind bill has raw sienna cast.
Tail and wings	Same as on canvasback drake.
Vermiculation	On tail area, sides and back, white, raw umber and Grumbacher gray; wash of raw umber.
Tertials	Paint this section of feathers a mix of raw umber, white, and a small amount of burnt umber; airbrush in centers by darkening previous mix with black; lighten edges with white and raw umber; also can use this mix for dots on adult bird.
Speculum	Thalo silver, small amounts of black and burnt umber; black and burnt umber for blackish edges; white on other edges, then dots.

Canvasback Hen
1984

Canvasback Hen
1984

2¼" Thick

Scale: 1" on this pattern equals 2" on full size pattern

HARLEQUIN DRAKE 1982

Sides	Two to three thin coats of yellow ochre; then a 3-to-1-to-1 mix of burnt sienna (Liquitex), cobalt blue, and burnt umber; if too dark, lighten with a wash of straight sienna.
Blue area: head, breast, back, and top part of tail	Mix ultramarine blue and burnt sienna for bluish cast, then add small amounts of white; add raw umber and black for desired shade; put on all feather tips with white and raw umber; then washes of original blue mix (may need additional washes of Grumbacher gray, black, raw umber, and ultramarine blue).
Head	For purplish cast, use Grumbacher purple wash on cheek, over eyes, and under chin; center of crown is black with white feather tips.
Rump, top of tail	Top of tail is blackish brown, more black than brown; under tail is black; white feather tips; then washes of burnt umber.
Speculum	For blue, use thalo blue and thalo green, then darken with black; can use iridescent blue.
Tertials	Three tertial feathers have brownish cast on outside; burnt umber washes on top of white feather tips.
Feet	Grayish blue color is a mix of white and Grumbacher gray, then washes of burnt umber; matte medium varnish.
Bill	Base coat bluish gray (entire bill); mix Grumbacher gray into white; darken toward base of bill; just add more Grumbacher gray; airbrush nail area—yellow into white; if too much contrast from dark to light, apply a couple thin washes of first shade of blue/gray; under the bill is darker.

The harlequin drake is a blue duck with distinct white markings.

The white markings, though unusual, are symmetrical.

These patches are really a chestnut white. The bill is a bluish gray.

Here can be studied the side pocket feather groupings.

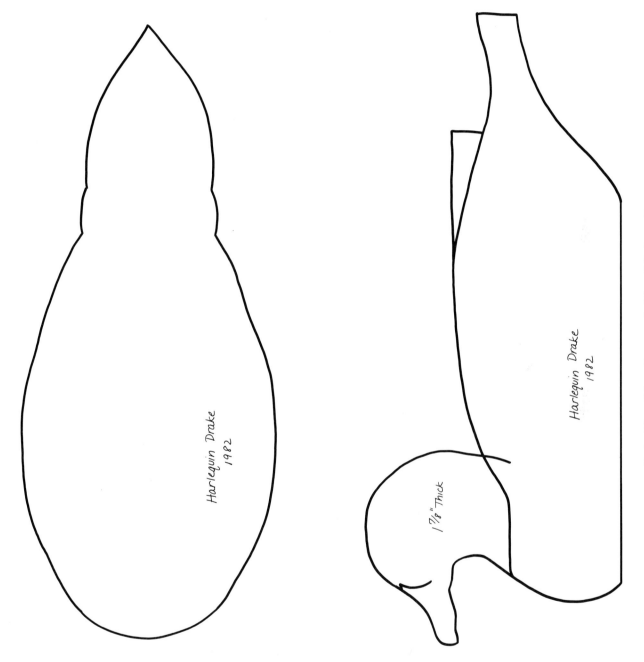

Harlequin Drake
1982

Harlequin Drake
1982

1 7/8" Thick

Scale: 1" on this pattern equals 2" on full-size pattern.

HOODED MERGANSER DRAKE   1978

Undercoat

Deft and thin gesso.

1st step

Mix Payne's gray into white for gray; paint thin coats over breast, lower sides, and under rump; white feather tips; thin washes of straight white until desired shade is reached; can paint white head section a straight white.

2nd step

Paint front a mix of yellow ochre and white watered in; then a mix of burnt sienna and ultramarine blue for back two-thirds of sides, watered into front one-third and lower sides; use burnt umber for washes and feather shading; vermiculate with a mix of black and burnt umber.

3rd step

Paint back, wings, and tail area burnt sienna, raw umber, and ultramarine blue; white feather tips on center section only (brownish area).

Vermiculation

Two parts black to one part burnt umber; then washes of raw umber for desired shade.

Head

For center of crown a mix of raw umber, white, and burnt sienna; black is a mix of ultramarine blue and burnt sienna.

Revisions 1980
Sides

Front half a shade of gray into yellowish shade; yellowish shade a mix of yellow ochre and white put on whole area; back two-thirds a mix of burnt sienna, cobalt blue, and yellow ochre; can darken with burnt umber and raw umber. Vermiculate with #0 Rapidograph pen; washes of raw umber if washes necessary; then apply matte medium varnish.

Long tertials

Dark greenish cast (Hooker's green and black).

This hooded merganser drake has a distinctive white patch on its head. Note also the shape of the head and bill.

A stoning attachment cuts in the separations on the back of the head. They are then redefined with a burning pen.

Note the vermiculation on the side pockets and the two distinctive vertical bars.

Note the feather flow and splits on the sides.

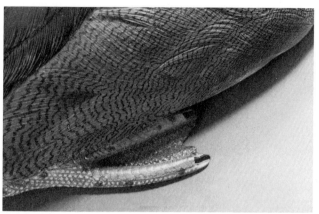

Here can be studied the rump and tertials. Also note that the vermicula-tion gets finer as you move toward the breast.

This leg was made of basswood.

A rear view of the bird shows the crossed pri-maries and where they are inserted.

Here is a good view of the back for feather layout and positioning of the head.

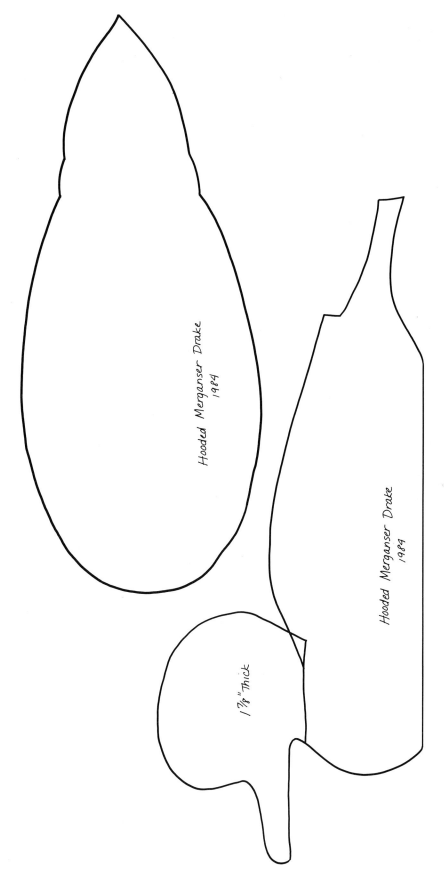

Hooded Merganser Drake
1984

Hooded Merganser Drake
1984

1⅞" Thick

Scale: 1" on this pattern equals 2" on full-size pattern.

HOODED MERGANSER HEN   1982

1st step	Deft spray; two coats with no steel-wooling (trying for a soft effect).
2nd step	Put white on lower breast and sides and under rump – this is gesso and small amount of raw umber mix.
3rd step	Put base coat on back, upper and lower rump area, and wings – a mix of burnt sienna and ultramarine blue and small amounts of burnt umber and white. Flick white on all feather tips of breast and sides (white and small amount of Grumbacher gray and raw umber); then from base out use a mix of burnt umber, white, and small amount of black, then washes of same; also can use a wash of black if tips need be darker; also a wash of raw sienna last, but on sides only.
Breast	From base out a darker shade of what was applied at base of breast – white, small amounts of burnt umber, and black.
Back, upper and lower rump	Flick white on all feather tips (white and small amount of raw umber); base out is raw umber, burnt umber, and small amount of black; rump area is darker.
Tail	Black on feather tips, then washes of black; black quills and white feather tips.
Tertials	White (white and raw umber) with green shading (Hooker's green and black).
Head	Work from white area forward; white area a mix of white, raw umber, burnt umber, and small amount of raw sienna watered into white; then washes of raw sienna, small amounts of white, and burnt umber watered into white area; lower portions of head have burnt sienna cast; use a grayish brown color for remainder of head; mix burnt umber, white, and small amount of black; don't forget whitish area under bill and corners of mouth; flick white on all feather tips; then wash with mousy color and one wash of black and/or Grumbacher gray.
Bill	Gesso and re-pencil crevices; lower area a mix of white, yellow ochre, and burnt umber watered in; then dark area on top of bill a blackish brown (ultramarine blue and burnt sienna).
Feet and legs	A mix of yellow ochre, small amounts of white and burnt umber; for darker webs add black and burnt umber, mostly burnt umber; also water in black spots; nails are black.

This hooded merganser hen is basically brown, with distinctive white feather edges. Also to be observed are the tail feathers that lay low in the water.

This photo gives a good view of the breast feathers.

Note the attitude of the head. The teeth in the bill are made from a coping saw blade cut to size.

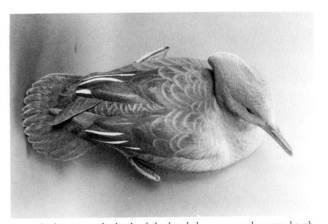

Here the layout on the back of the hooded merganser hen can be observed.

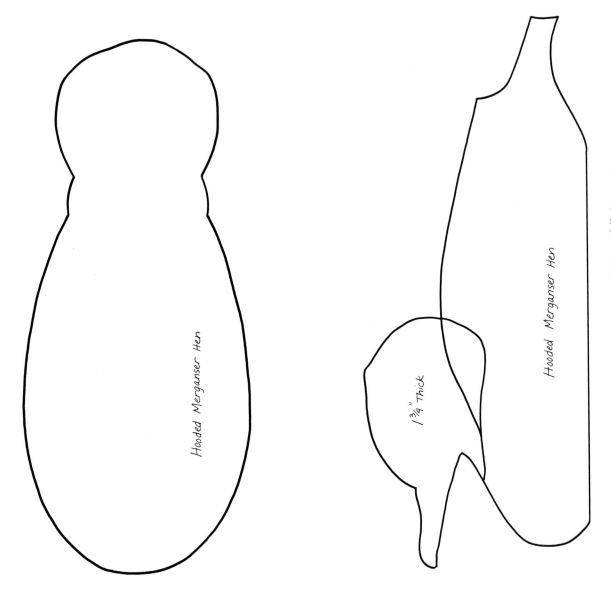

Hooded Merganser Hen

Hooded Merganser Hen

1¾" Thick

Scale: 1" on this pattern equals 2" on full-size pattern.

REDHEAD DRAKE   1980

Start with vermiculated area	Thin coats of white and Grumbacher gray and small amounts of raw umber; put white on lower half of sides and on feather tips; then light coat of burnt umber from base out.
Breast and rump area	Ultramarine blue and burnt sienna (black); then white feather tips; burnt umber on all feather tips; washes of straight black on breast and burnt umber on rump area.
Head	First, bring feather tips into black area of breast with gesso; then a thin wash of gesso and yellow ochre before applying burnt sienna, cobalt blue, and burnt umber mix; back of neck and lower neck a purplish shade (Grumbacher purple or Liquitex dioxazine purple); if too dull looking, use a thin wash of Grumbacher red.
Tail	Burnt umber, white, and small amount of black; darker quills; white feather tips; then wash with straight black.
Tertials	First a mix of raw umber, burnt umber, and small amounts of white and black; blend into back area; darken center with burnt umber, raw umber, and small amount of black; make quills darker by using same mix with more black; white feather tips (white and raw umber); can use a wash of raw umber and burnt umber for desired shade.
Speculum	Gesso first; thalo silver, small amount of black and burnt umber; black washes; black edges are ultramarine blue and burnt sienna; white on lower feather tips.
Vermiculation	A mix of raw umber, burnt umber, and ultramarine blue or black. Remember: the finer (closer) the vermiculation, the lighter the base coat should be. Under the rump area, vermiculate with straight raw umber (shade with raw umber from base out on all feathers before vermiculating).
Bill	Gesso—then bluish gray; first white—small amount of Grumbacher gray, then add small amounts of ultramarine blue and burnt umber; second white—white and Grumbacher gray; band—straight white.

Redhead Drake - 1983 World Pairs

Redhead Drake - 1983 World Pairs

Scale: 1" on this pattern equals 2" on full-size pattern.

REDHEAD HEN   1983

Undercoat

Gesso with small amounts of raw umber, yellow ochre, burnt umber (thin coats); mix white and raw umber for belly area and under tip of tail.

Sides, breast, and a couple rows of feathers behind neck

Apply a mix of raw umber, burnt umber, small amount of yellow ochre and white (washes); then darken this mix with ultramarine blue and put on back, rump and tail; flick white on feather tips where needed (white, raw umber, and raw sienna).

Back area

Mix burnt umber into yellow ochre, then add raw umber and ultramarine blue to darken; can use a small amount of white to lighten; darken from base out by adding black; then flick white (white, small amount of black and burnt umber) on tips (they should have a silvery look); center of tertial feathers is burnt umber, raw umber, and ultramarine blue watered in.

Breast

White (white and raw umber) on feather tips, then raw sienna, burnt umber, and raw umber from base out; do this all the way to the white tips, then come back with darker color (burnt umber, raw umber, and ultramarine blue) from base out; with brush draw white and dark lines through the feathers.

Head

Thin coats of gesso and raw umber; then two thin coats of white, burnt umber, raw umber, and black for a cream color; water in a mix of burnt umber, raw umber, yellow ochre, and burnt sienna; darken crown with ultramarine blue and burnt sienna; white feather tips are white and raw umber; the washes of second color mix for crown.

Speculum

First gesso; then a mix of Payne's gray and iridescent silver for base color; make tips darker by adding more burnt umber and black; black tips and white on lowest feather area; then one wash of burnt umber and one wash of black (thin); this can never be too thin; better to have two thin coats than one wash that is too dark.

Tail and wings

Burnt umber, white, and small amount of black for base color; white on feather tips (white and raw umber); black and burnt umber for quills; then thin washes of black.

Bill

Base coat a mix of black, white, and Payne's gray; this is a darker shade than drake; darker around edge of bill next to face.

Redhead Hen - 1983 World Prs.

Redhead Hen - 1983 World Prs.

2¼" Thick

Scale: 1" on this pattern equals 2" on full-size pattern.

RING-NECKED DUCK DRAKE 1984

Undercoat	Deft and gesso.
Sides	Grumbacher gray, white, and small amount of raw umber; add white feather tips after breast is completed.
Breast	Paint a mix of burnt sienna and ultramarine blue; then straight black feather tips followed by straight black washes.
Head	Gesso (into breast); put three to four thin washes of Grumbacher purple or dioxazine purple and black; airbrush ivory black on crown behind bill, under chin and back of neck, then airbrush Hooker's green on crown; airbrush ring around neck with burnt sienna and burnt umber; flick small feather tips (white and raw umber) back from bill approximately one-quarter to one-half inch; don't forget white under bill; purple iridescent mix on head.
Back, tail area, under rump, and wings	Paint area burnt sienna, ultramarine blue; apply black under tail area; straight black on all feather tips, then washes of straight black; then apply Hooker's green and small amount of black; thalo green on last tertial feather.
Speculum	Silver greenish cast – thalo silver, small amount of black, burnt umber, then thin black washes; white on leading edges.
Vermiculation	#00 ink pen; fix vermiculation with matte spray; washes of white; splits of white; can use burnt umber for shadows on sides.
Bill	Gesso; thin coats of white, ultramarine blue or Grumbacher gray, and burnt umber over entire bill, feet and legs; white areas next – white (small amount of gesso, white, and raw umber); black is burnt sienna and ultramarine blue; varnish.
Feet and legs	Bluish gray – white, Grumbacher gray, ultramarine blue, and burnt umber; blackish nails, spots, and webs.

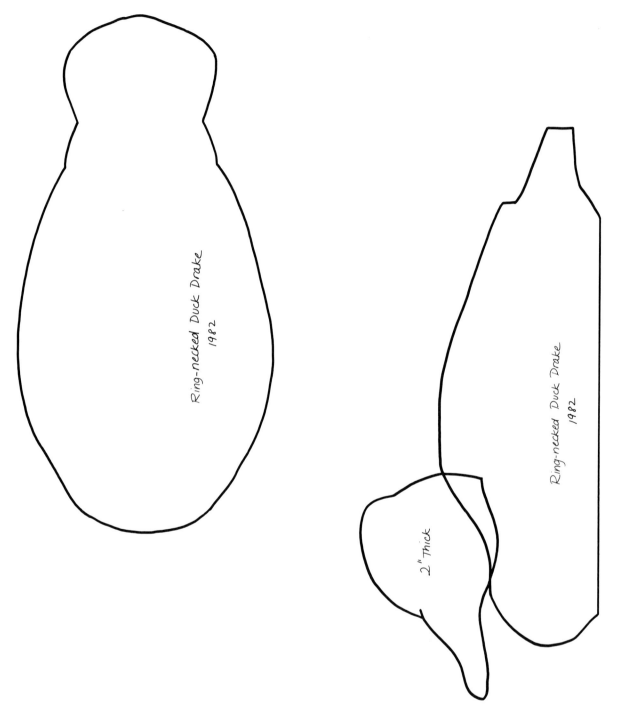

Ring-necked Duck Drake
1982

Ring-necked Duck Drake
1982

2" Thick

Scale: 1" on this pattern equals 2" on full-size pattern.

RING-NECKED DUCK HEN   1982

Undercoat	Deft and gesso.
1st step	For head and lower sides, use gesso, small amount of white, and raw umber.
2nd step	For breast, sides, and under tail area, use a mix of raw umber, raw sienna, and white; at this point suggest doing base color of back, top of tail, and wings (see below); flick white (white and raw umber) on all feather tips; sides darken from base out with base coat, darken breast with small amount of black; washes of raw sienna and raw umber, also a wash of black on breast; ink in all splits on breast; then matte medium varnish.
3rd step	For back, top of rump, tail, and wings, first apply a mix of burnt sienna (Hyplar) and ultramarine blue—four to five coats; darken from base out; tertials don't have white feather tips; darken these with greenish color from base out (thalo green and small amount of black); quills are black.
	For tail and wing feather tips, black, then washes of black; speculum is thalo silver, black, and small amount of thalo green; black washes; black feather tips.
4th step	Paint entire head a grayish shade—black base, and small amounts of white and raw umber—three or four thin coats, watering in white area around eyes and under chin; crown darker (burnt sienna, ultramarine blue, and small amount of burnt umber) watered into gray; back of neck reddish brown; flick white (white, raw umber, and Grumbacher gray) on cheeks and crown; put washes of grayish shade on cheeks, then burnt umber on crown—first with brush, then washes; black wash for final finish.
5th step	Paint entire bill dark gray shade (white, Grumbacher gray, and burnt umber); white next (white and small amount of Grumbacher gray); black on tip (burnt sienna, ultramarine blue, and small amount of black).

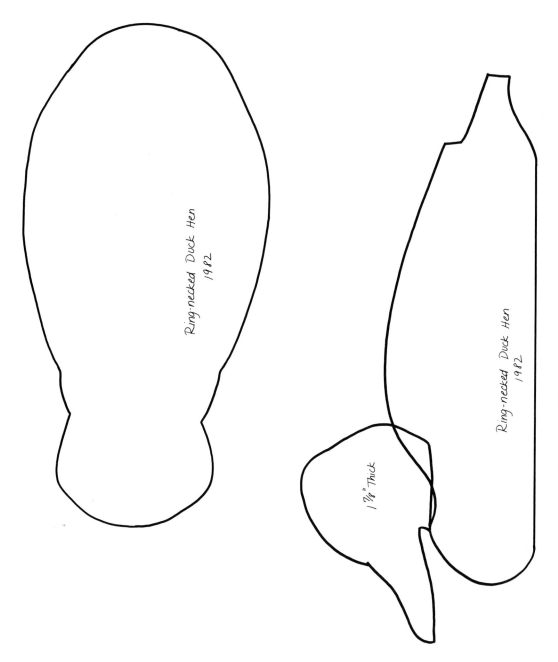

Ring-necked Duck Hen
1982

Ring-necked Duck Hen
1982

1 7/8" Thick

Scale: 1" on this pattern equals 2" on full-size pattern.

RUDDY DUCK DRAKE 1984

1st step	Two to three thin coats of Deft spray to seal (Colonial Maple); if reddish tone desired, add some burnt sienna to the gesso.
2nd step	Apply two thin washes of yellow ochre on red area of bird.
3rd step	For rust color, mix burnt sienna with cobalt blue or ultramarine blue in 3-to-1 mix.
4th step	The breast feathers are flicked or edged with burnt sienna and ultramarine blue; then a thin wash of burnt umber to tone down the area; with #1 or #0 brush, highlight splits with black and burnt umber mix; lower third breast feathers can be tipped with white and raw umber.
5th step	Side pockets and wing and back feathers edged lightly with yellow ochre; finish with washes of burnt umber and the mix from 4th step; highlight splits with black-burnt umber mix.
6th step	For top of tail feathers, use washes of burnt sienna with ultramarine blue and a small amount of white; paint quills and edges of feathers with black; finish with thin wash of black or burnt umber; bottom of tail feathers lighter — use washes of burnt sienna, ultramarine blue, and white; edge feather tips with white; quills raw sienna; finish with a thin wash of black or burnt umber.
7th step	Outline white area on head very lightly with pencil dots; paint with washes of white plus a small amount of Payne's gray; use white only to edge feather tips; then several thin washes until desired shade is reached.
	For the cape, mix ultramarine blue with burnt sienna in 2-to-1 ratio, plus a small amount of black; highlight feather edges with white plus raw umber; finish with washes of black and burnt sienna in 2-to-1 ratio.
8th step	Paint rump with thin washes of white and burnt umber; then washes of white and gray; highlight feather tips at random with white near the top, and with burnt umber and the mix from 3rd step for the feathers near the bottom; finish with washes of white.
9th step	For the bill, paint underside and top with a pink mix of white plus red and small amount of burnt umber or black; follow with thin washes of burnt umber or black; tip of bill should be a bit more whitish; paint nail and some of the front curve of the bill black.
10th step	Paint bill with matte medium to give waxy appearance; paint quills with matte medium and varnish (Hyplar).

Made in 1981, this is the first ruddy duck Jim carved.

Seen here are the ruddy duck's breast feather patterns and face details.

The bill is a light blue with distinctive depressions.

Here is a good detail of the side pocket.

The tail of the ruddy duck drake is in courtship display.

For study in this photo are the layout of the back and the positioning of the head.

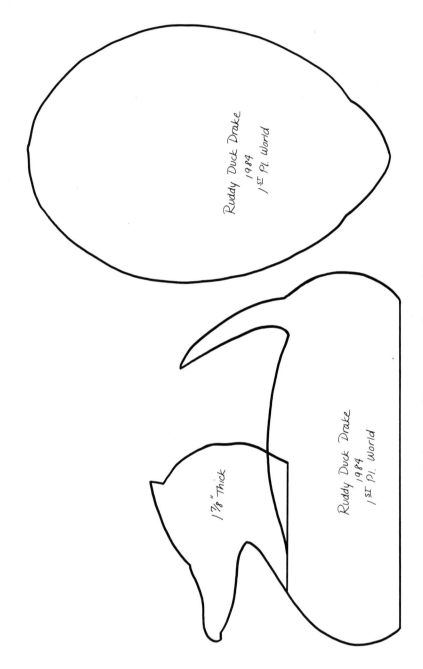

Ruddy Duck Drake
1984
1ST Pl. World

Ruddy Duck Drake
1984
1ST Pl. World

1⅞" Thick

Scale: 1" on this pattern equals 2" on full-size pattern.

7

Field Notes for Marsh and Diving Ducks

Black Duck Drake

The body, except the head, has a dark brown cast with creamy white to burnt umber feather tips; these tips can vary greatly in color. Remember that each breast feather has a U-shaped marking of the same color as the feather tip. The head is a creamy white with a definite streaked pattern of dark brown/black; crown and through the eye area a dark brown/black. Eyes are dark brown. Bill is yellow to olive green; nail is black; top of bill can be a light yellow on adult drake. Speculum is a metallic purplish blue, often with white on the feather tips. Feet can range in color from red/orange to a dirty-looking red with darker webs.

Baikal Teal Drake

The sides and breast are like those of the green-winged teal. Chest is buff, dotted with black spots. Sides are gray with wavy lines: note white sidebar that extends into white belly. Scapulars are chestnut, buff, and black. Head has black crown and hindneck and two buff patches in front of and behind the eyes; a curving line on the back of the head and neck is metallic green and white. The wings are brown. Speculum is green, edged with white and reddish brown. Eyes are dark brown.

Blue-winged Teal Drake

Breast, belly, and sides have a pale red to pale yellow appearance with round, black spots forming bars on the upper sides; flanks are white. Head and neck are a slate blue/gray color with green and purplish areas behind the eyes. Crown and chin are black with white, half-moons in front of the eyes; this white can extend well behind the eyes on adult birds. Bill is black to bluish-black. Eyes are brown. Feet are a dirty yellow with black webs. Tertials have a greenish, flat black color with centers a yellow/buff color. Wing coverts are a cobalt blue tipped with white. Speculum is a metallic to iridescent green.

Cinnamon Teal Drake

Sides are cinnamon red; flanks have a yellowish cast. Head, neck, and breast are a much richer shade of cinnamon red; crown is black. Eyes are orange/red. Bill is black and always appears to be longer than the head. Back is dusky brown (raw umber appearance) with cinnamon-colored markings and edges on lower portion and sides; straight brown edges on feathers toward center. Rump, lower breast, and belly are brownish/black. Legs and feet are yellowish-orange; webs a dusky color. Wings (lesser and middle coverts) are cobalt blue; greater coverts are white with inner coverts a brownish blue, tipped with white. Tertials are blackish green on lower half; upper half a brownish black striped with a reddish yellow buff. Speculum is a metallic to iridescent green.

Cinnamon Teal Hen and Blue-winged Teal Hen

Back, sides, breast, and rump area have a dark brown appearance with feather tips of buff – a bit more of a raw sienna cast on the cinnamon teal hen. The belly is white. Legs and feet are the same as those of the drakes. Wings for both are the same – similar to cinnamon teal drake except the blue of the lesser and middle coverts is duller; greater coverts more slate-colored, tipped with white. Speculum is a blackish green tipped with white. Tertials are same brown as basic body color with lighter buff edges. Head has a greenish to off-white color with streaked face pattern of black/brown. Crown is darker with a dark area extending from bill through the eyes; chin, throat, and under base of bill are off-white. Bill is larger on the cinnamon teal hen. Eyes are brown.

Gadwall Drake

The body appears gray; the back and sides are a dark, brownish black with fine vermiculation of buff/white. Chest appears to have a black cast with the same buffy white, crescent scales. Head is a cream to gray color with darker black/brown streaks – different from those on the black duck. Crown is darker, being chestnut toward the bill and a blackish color on the back of the neck. Eyes are brown to reddish brown. Bill has a cast of bluish black, with the lower part of the upper mandible yellow-orange. Rump has a greenish black cast. Belly is an off-white. Feet are a yellowish orange with webs a dusky black. Middle coverts are a chestnut color; greater coverts are black. Tertials are light gray with tips usually off-white.

Green-winged Teal Drake

Sides and back have a grayish cast, with brownish-black vermiculation. Chest is a pink buff color with irregular black spots. The head is a brownish chestnut color with yellowish green patch; it is a black to dark blue in front of the eyes and at the nape. Note the creamy line of feathers from the base of bill which separates the dark brown crown and green area. Bill has a black to black/brown (leathery) look. Eyes are brown. Feet are bluish gray, the same as the hen's. Speculum is jet black to a metallic green as is the hen's; black feathers usually have white/buff tips with a row of brownish-raw sienna color bordering the front of the speculum. Don't forget to paint on vertical white bars between the breast and sides.

Green-winged Teal Hen

The smallest of all North American ducks; its overall body is dusky brown with light feather tips. Head is shaped the same as drake's, only without the crest. Color is whitish to buff with streaked pattern; it's a darker, dusky brown through the eyes, with a cream-colored area right behind the bill and under the chin. Eyes are brown. Bill is purplish gray with blackish spots on lower part; the top is blackish. Feet are gray to blue gray; webs a dusky color. Lower breast and belly are mottled on pale gray. Speculum is jet black to metallic green; black feathers usually have white/buff tips with a bar of a brownish/raw sienna color in front of the speculum.

Pintail Drake

Body has a gray cast with black vermiculation. Chest and belly are white. Rump area usually has a yellowish patch on both sides. Tail has two long middle feathers; these have a greenish metallic cast. The rest of the tail feathers are brownish gray with off-white feather tips. Speculum has a cast of green and bronze, bordered by black, then white, feather tips. Tertials are gray with bright black stripes. Feet are grayish blue with black webs. Eyes are dark brown. Bill is blue-gray with black along the ridge; there is also a black nail and black at the corner of the upper mandible. Head is dark brown, and a metallic pink and green is visible. Crown is a darker brown/black color. Back of neck is black and blends into the gray of the back.

Pintail Hen

Back, sides, and rump have a dark brown cast with buff-to-cream colored-feather tips. Breast is a buff brown with dark brown feather patterns. Head is the same buff cast with dark brown feather patterns on the face. The crown is darker. Chin and throat are usually off-white. Bill is a blue gray. Eyes are dark brown. Feet are the same as the drake's. Speculum is similar to the drake's, only duller and spotted with black.

Shoveler Drake

Breast and foreback are white; back is a raw umber shade of black, with lighter feather edges. Head and neck are iridescent green, depending on how light hits the head; shades of blue are often visible. Crown is brownish/black. Bill is black; the lower mandible is usually lighter; lamellae are usually a dirty shade of pink. The widest part of bill is around 1¼ inches. Eyes are yellow. Scapulars are white; larger ones have a greenish/black color; others a shade of cobalt blue. Belly is a chestnut color with large white patch in front of the tail. Rump is black with a green cast close to that of the tail's top and bottom. Legs and feet are orange. Center feathers of tail are light brown with off-white edges; feathers get white toward the sides. Wings (lesser and middle coverts) are cobalt blue; greater coverts grayish with white tips. Speculum is a metallic green to iridescent green, bordered in front with white bars. Tertials are a greenish black, streaked with white.

Shoveler Hen

Back, sides, breast, and rump area have a brown cast with feather tips a buff color (top sides a yellowish cast). Head and neck are grayish buff to off-white, streaked with a black/brown color; crown and area through the eyes is darker; throat and base of bill without streaks. Bill is olive to olive brown, turning a green shade toward the tip; it has black spots, and lower mandible is orange. Eyes are yellow. Feet and legs are orange. Wings (lesser and middle coverts) are

grayish blue. Speculum is not as metallic green as the drake's; it is bordered in front and behind with white.

Wood Duck Drake

Back and tail area have a metallic green cast; chest has a purple/chestnut color with an off-white cone-shaped pattern. Sides are lemon color with black vermiculation. Top of side pockets have black and white feather tips. Eyes are red to red/orange with red eyelids. Head has different iridescent colors, starting with a green metallic crown which blends into an iridescent blue, then purplish black; cheeks have areas of iridescent purple, green and bronze. The neck is black with white chin and throat areas. Very distinct white feather patterns are found on the head. Check reference on bill, as it is unusual: short with distinct black nail; bill has red, black, and white colors. Also note black and white vertical feather pattern between chestnut breast and sides. Legs and feet are dirty yellow with blackish webs. Rump area is a bronzy green. Tertials are black with white tips on the inner ones; outer tertials are black with hues of metallic blue.

Bufflehead Drake

Chest and sides are white; upper feathers on sides have black edges. Back is black and may have a few feathers with white tips. Rump is black, turning into gray on the sides. Head and upper neck are black with purple, green, and violet; below each eye, a white patch extends up and over the hind crown; lower neck is white. Bill is blue gray, and may have a yellowish portion on upper mandible; nail, tip, and base are dusky black. Eyes are brown. Breast and belly are white to an ash gray. Legs and feet are flesh pink with black claws. Tail is a dark gray; outer feathers usually have white tips. All coverts are white with a few dark feathers along the forward edges of the wings.

Canvasback Drake

Chest and foreback are brownish black. Back and scapulars are white with a fine vermiculation of faded blackish brown – much whiter than on the redhead drake. Rump area is brownish black, the same as the chest. Head and neck are reddish chestnut, but darker on the crown and behind the bill and throat. Bill is black. Eyes are red. Belly is white. Legs and feet are grayish blue with darker webs. Tail is slate brown.

Wings are also slate brown, but darker on the tips. The speculum is pearl gray, shading into a white bar behind; outer edges of inner secondaries have black margins. Tertials are white, vermiculated with a dusky color.

Canvasback Hen

Chest and foreback are reddish to a yellow brown. Back, sides, and scapulars are whitish, barred and marked with slate brown color. Rump is a dusky brown. Breast is an off-white; belly is grayish brown. Legs and feet are the same as the drake's. Head and neck are reddish to yellow brown with darker crown; chin, throat, and area behind the eyes are an off-white. Bill is same as the drake's. Eyes are brown. Tail is brownish. Wings are brownish gray, darker on the tips and the outer webs. Speculum is a pearl gray.

Harlequin Drake

Chest and foreback a slate blue; white crescent bordered with black in front of wing bend. Scapulars and hindback are slate blue with white middle feathers. Rump is a darker slate blue (almost black). Breast is brown; belly is same color as breast but slightly darker. Sides are reddish brown with a small white spot near the base of the tail. Head and neck are slate blue; the crown is black; a white patch before the eye turns into a reddish chestnut above the eye and continues to the back of the neck. There is also a white spot below and behind each eye. A third white mark (stripe) on each side of the neck runs around the lower portion of the neck. Bill is bluish gray with a yellowish nail. Eye is dark brown, and may even have a reddish cast. Legs and feet are grayish blue with darker webs. Tail is pointed, black in color with black upper and under coverts. Wings are slate in color; greater coverts have a purplish cast with a series of small white spots in front of the speculum. Speculum is dark blue. Primaries are blackish to brown on the inner webs.

Hooded Merganser Drake

Foreback is black with the hindback and rump a dark brown. Scapulars are black. Chest and breast are white. Sides are reddish brown vermiculated with black; heavier vermiculation at the rear. Belly is white with two black bars going from foreback diagonally downward into sides of chest. Head is black; forehead usually has a brownish cast. Crest, which has hairlike appearance, is white bordered with black: this white area resembles a fan. Neck is glossy black. Bill is black with a cylindrical hook across the entire top of the bill. Eyes are yellow. Legs and feet are olive yellow to light brown; webs are darker, brownish black. Tail is dark brown. Under coverts are grayish brown with white specks; lesser coverts are blackish and tipped with gray; middle coverts are gray; greater coverts are dusky-colored to white. Primaries are black on outer webs and tips; inner webs are lighter in color. Tertials are black, or occasionally a greenish cast, striped with white.

Hooded Merganser Hen

Back and scapulars are brownish black; rump is darker. Chest and sides are gray with off-white tips. Breast and belly are white to off-white. Head is grayish brown (a mousy color) with a darker crown; crest is reddish brown, usually whitish at the rear; rear feathers are hairlike. Neck is mousy gray. Chin and throat are off-white. The upper mandible of bill is black with dark orange on the edge; lower mandible is a dirty yellow; nail is black. Eyes are yellow to brown. Legs and feet are greenish brown with black webs. Tail is brownish black. Wings are brown to ash brown with white tips; primaries same as the drake's. Tertials are blackish with off-white stripes.

Redhead Drake

Chest and foreback are black; lighter feather tips on lower part. Back, sides, and scapulars are vermiculated, giving a dark gray or metallic shade. Head and neck are chestnut/red with a purplish area on the neck. Bill is a light blue with an off-white ring bordering a black tip. Eyes are orange to orange yellow. Legs and feet are bluish gray with dusky webs. Tail is blackish brown. Speculum is pearl gray. All wing coverts are gray and slightly flecked with white. Tertials are gray.

Redhead Hen

Back, rump, and scapulars grayish brown finely speckled with white. Chest has brownish feathers with off-white tips. Sides have brownish feathers tipped with off white. Breast is off white shaded into a gray brown on the belly. Legs and feet same as drake, but a bit less color. Head is yellowish brown, darker on the crown, paler at the base of the bill and under chin; has a faint, palish streak behind eyes and a ring around the eyes. Bill same as drake, but usually not as bright in color. Eyes are brown. Tail is grayish brown. Coverts also grayish brown. Wings brownish gray, but darker on tips. Speculum is pearl gray. Tertials are brownish gray.

Ring-necked Duck Drake

Chest, back, and rump area are black. Scapulars are black with a greenish cast. Belly sides are gray to silver with fine, dusky vermiculation. Head and neck are black with purple iridescence; crown sometimes has a greenish cast; a chestnut ring circles the lower neck. On the chin behind the bill is a white triangular patch. The bill is dark slate gray with narrow white edges at the base; a white ring surrounds the bill near the black tip. Eyes are straw to yellow color. Legs and feet are grayish blue with blackish webs. Tail is a slate brown. Wing coverts are grayish brown with a greenish cast. Primaries are brownish black, darker on the tips. Speculum is pearl gray.

Ring-necked Duck Hen

The lower back and rump are reddish brown to a darker shade. Scapulars are reddish brown; longer ones usually are darker with a greenish cast. Chest and sides have brown feathers edged with white. Breast is white, mottled with brownish gray, becoming a darker brown on the belly. Head is grayish brown, darker on the crown; cheeks are a light brown; chin, throat and area around base of the bill are whitish. The nape is rusty brown; the foreneck is grayish brown. There is an off-white ring around and behind the eyes, which are brown. Bill is the same as the drake's. Tail is dark brown. Wing coverts are grayish brown. Primaries are blackish brown, but darker on the tips. Speculum is pearl gray.

Ruddy Duck Drake (Summer Plumage)

Back, chest, sides, rump, scapulars, and foreback are reddish chestnut color. Breast is a silvery white. Hindback is dark brown. Crown and nape are black to just below the eye, which is outlined with white cheek; chin is also white. Neck, which is short and heavy, is reddish chestnut. Bill is a bright blue with the tip curving upward; underpart of lower mandible is a flesh color. Eyes are brown. Legs and feet are bluish gray with blackish webs. Tail is blackish brown. Upper coverts are chestnut; under coverts are white. All wing coverts are dark brown. Primaries, tertials, and secondaries are also dark brown with fine specks of lighter brown.

Appendix

1147 Golden Olive Court
Sanibel Island, FL 33957
(813) 472-8666   fax: (813) 472-8445

Dear Carver:

Starting in 1995, our seminars will be conducted at two new locations. One will be on Sanibel Island at Tarpon Bay, Florida, next to the world-renowned "Ding" Darling Wildlife Refuge. This teaching facility, which is leased to us under the auspices of the Sanibel-Captiva Conservation Foundation, sits on a tropical lagoon, is fully air-conditioned, and is next to a canoe/fishing-guide operation. Our northern location will be at the new Queen Anne's County Arts Council facility in Centreville, Maryland, very near our original site on Kent Island.

My carving sessions will explore use of research and reference material, laying out patterns and roughing out the bird, laying out feather groupings, texturing and stoning, positioning of eyes, and final preparation of birds for painting. My painting sessions will focus on use of acrylic paints, demonstration of blending and feather flicking, application of iridescents, and sequences in painting the bird.

All classes will begin with an introductory session on Sunday evening and may continue until Saturday noon, depending upon the size of the project. For those of you needing accommodations, we will send you a list of suggested motels—rates begin at about $35 per night, including tax. Both locations, Sanibel and Centreville, have RV and camper facilities nearby.

You will be responsible for your own breakfast and evening meals, and we will furnish you with lunch each day, as well as coffee and tea. Soft drinks are available at a nominal fee. Thursday evening we will conduct an open discussion group on class progress toward the week's goals. We will host your evening meal during this discussion, and your spouse is invited to join us at this time.

The closest airport to the Centreville, Maryland, location is Baltimore/Washington International at Baltimore; the closest airport to Sanibel is Regional Southwest Airport in Ft. Myers. We will be glad to arrange for a pick-up *at these two airports only,* so please keep that in mind when making your travel arrangements.

To reserve a space during the week of your choice, contact us at our new address. Reservations are $50; after you have made a reservation, we will send you an invoice for the remainder of the tuition, which is due sixty days before the class starts. Excluding the deposit, all tuitions will be refunded if cancellations are made before thirty days prior to the beginning of the session. Other refunds are made on a case-by-case basis.

Upon receipt of the tuition, we will send you a list of carving/painting tools and materials needed for your specific class, directions to the class workshop, and the names and addresses of those attending your same session. A basic wood cutout will be supplied for carving, and in Jim's painting classes, a molded study bird will be furnished. We have carving and painting supplies, books, molded birds, and other supplies for sale here.

Because each class has only eleven students, we can accommodate any level of expertise, from beginner to advanced, but the downside is that classes may fill up quickly, so we urge you to send in your deposit as soon as you have made your choice. If there are any questions regarding these seminars, *please feel free to call or write us—Jim or Patty—we are always available.*

Many of our former students have expressed dismay and shock that we have moved from our original location on Kent Island, and while we have been contacted by eager learners in the Southeast section of the country, some alumni have shown a certain resistance to making the move with us. To those of you, I would like to say that we have deliberately selected our dates with lower off-season air rates in mind. As well, we have found accommodations similar in caliber to those we had used in the Kent Island area, *at similar prices.* And these motels on Sanibel are all on the Gulf of Mexico with swimming pools—no more traffic noise of Route 50! Sanibel is twenty to thirty minutes closer to the airport than our Maryland classroom was to BWI.

At Tarpon Bay the location of the classroom itself is so beautiful, in a secluded cove shaded by palm trees with a constant Gulf breeze, that you will wonder how you can return to civilization. For those accompanied by spouses, we will be happy to furnish you information on all the shopping, shelling, swimming, and cultural activities available on the Island. We could even take a class tour through the Wildlife Refuge. So, we hope that our former students will be receptive to our new location. We are excited about it, and believe that it is a good move for us and for Greenwing University. For those of you who think Florida is too hot, remember those mid-summer days on the Chesapeake! The National Weather Service is on record as saying that summers are hotter on the Chesapeake (Washington/Baltimore) than they are here.

Sincerely,

Jim Sprankle

P.S. Over the years our feedback has consistently told us that many people want to come, but are intimidated by what they perceive to be their lack of ability. This should not be a concern. The format of our classes is specifically designed to accommodate both the novice and the more advanced student. We will furnish you upon request with names of graduates (in your area if possible) so that you may contact them directly and discuss any apprehension you may have about your skill level.

Sources for Supplies

Al's Decoy Supplies
27 Connaught Ave.
London, Ontario N5Y 3A4
CANADA
519-451-4729

American Sales Co.
Box 741
Reseda, CA 91335
213-881-2808

Canadian Woodworker Ltd.
1391 St. James St.
Winnipeg, Manitoba R3H 0Z1
CANADA 204-786-3196

Carvers Corner
153 Passaic St.
Garfield, NJ 07026
201-472-7511

Albert Constantine & Son, Inc.
2050 Eastchester Rd.
Bronx, NY 10461
718-792-1600
718-792-2110 (fax)

Craft Cove, Inc.
2315 W. Glen Ave.
Peoria, IL 61614
309-692-8365

CraftWoods
2101 Greenspring Dr.
Timonium, MD 21093
410-561-9469
410-560-0760 (fax)

Curt's Waterfowl Corner
P.O. Box 228
123 Le Boeuf St.
Montegut, LA 70377
504-594-3012
504-594-2328 (fax)
1-800-523-8474 (orders)

The Duck Butt Boys
327 Rosedown Way
Mandeville, LA 70448
504-626-8919

Electric & Tool Service Co.
19442 Conant Ave.
Detroit, MI 48234
313-366-3830
313-366-1855 (fax)

P.C. English Enterprises
6201 Mallard Rd., Box 380
Thornburg, VA 22565
703-582-2200

Exotic Woods, Inc.
2483 Industrial Street
Burlington, Ontario L7P 1A6
CANADA
905-335-8066
905-335-7080 (fax)

Feather Merchants
279 Boston Post Rd.
Madison, CT 06443
203-245-1231

The Foredom Electric Co.
16 Stony Hill Rd., Rt. 6
Bethel, CT 06801
203-792-8622
203-790-9832 (fax)

Forest Products
P.O. Box 12
Avon, OH 44011
216-937-5630

Garrett Wade
161 Avenue of the Americas
New York, NY 10013
1-800-212-2942

George Nelson, Inc.
2680 S. McKenzie
Foley, AL 36535
1-800-44-DUCKS

Jennings Decoy
601 Franklin Ave. NE
St. Cloud, MN 56304
612-253-2253
612-253-9537 (fax)

J.H. Kline Carving Shop
P.O. Box 445, Forge Hill Rd.
Manchester, PA 17345
717-266-3501

Lee Valley Tools Ltd.
1080 Morrisson Dr.
Ottawa, Ontario K2H 8K7
CANADA
613-596-0350
613-596-3073 (fax)

Lewis Tool and Supply Co.
912 West 8th St.
Loveland, CO 80537
303-663-4405

Little Mountain Supply Co.
Rt. 2, Box 1329
Front Royal, VA 22630
703-636-3125

Ritter Carvers
1559 Dillon Rd.
Maple Glen, PA 19002
215-646-4896

Ross Tool Co.
257 Queen Street, West
Toronto, Ontario M5V 1Z4
CANADA
416-598-2498

Tool Bin
10575 Clark Rd.
Davisburg, MI 48350
810-625-0390
810-546-1725 (fax)

Veasy Studios
182 Childs Rd.
Elkton, MD 21921
410-392-3850
410-392-2832 (fax)

Warren Tool Co.
2209-1 Rte 9G
Rhinebeck, NY 12572
914-876-7817

WASCO (Wildlife Artist Supply Co.)
1306 West Spring St.
P.O. Box 967
Monroe, GA 30655
1-800-334-8012
404-267-8970 (fax)

Welbeck Sawmill Ltd.
R.R. 2
Durham, Ontario N0G 2V0
CANADA
519-369-2144
519-369-3372 (fax)

Wildlife Carvings Supply
317 Holyoke Ave.
Beach Haven, NJ 08008
609-492-1871

Wildlife Woodcarvers
Avian Art, Inc.
4288 Staunton Dr.
Swartz Creek, MI 48473
313-732-6300

Wood Carvers Store and School
3056 Excelsior Blvd.
Minneapolis, MN 55416
612-927-7491
612-927-0324 (fax)

Woodcraft Supply Corp.
210 Wood County Industrial Park
Parkersburg, WV 26101
1-800-225-1153

Burning Tools
Annex Mfg.
955 Blue Ball Rd.
Elkton, MD 21921

Chesterfield Craft Shop
20 Georgetown Rd.
Trenton, NJ 08620
609-298-2015

Colwood Electronics
15 Meridian Rd.
Eatontown, NJ 07724
908-544-1119
908-544-1118 (fax)

Detail Master Burning Systems
2650 Davisson St.
River Grove, IL 60171
708-452-5400
708-453-7515 (fax)

Hot Tools, Inc.
24 Tioga Way
P.O. Box 615
Marblehead, MA 01945
617-639-1000
617-631-8887 (fax)

Carving Knives

Lominack Knives
P.O. Box 1189
Abingdon, VA 24212-1189
703-628-6591

Jack Andrews, Knives
1482 Maple Ave.
Paoli, PA 19301
610-644-6318

Cast Feet

See Chesterfield Craft Shop under "Burning Tools,"
above.

Richard Delise
920 Springwood Dr.
West Chester, PA 19382
610-436-4377

Taylor Made Bird Feet
165 Terrianne Dr.
Taunton, MA 02780
508-824-3337

Cast Study Bills

Bob Bolle
26421 Compson
Roseville, MI 48066
313-773-3153

Highwood Book Shop
P.O. Box 1246
Traverse City, MI 49685
616-271-3898

Bob Miller
General Delivery
Evergreen, LA 71333
318-346-4270

Oscar Johnston Wildlife Gallery
Rt. 2, Box 1224
Smith River, CA 95567
707-487-4401

Waterfowl Study Bills, Inc.
P.O. Box 310
Evergreen, LA 71333
318-346-4814
318-346-7633 (fax)

Glass Eyes

Carver's Eye Co.
P.O. Box 16692
Portland, OR 97216
503-666-5680 (fax same)

Eyes
9630 Dundalk
Spring, TX 77379
713-376-2897

Hutch Decoy Carving Ltd.
7715 Warsaw Ave.
Glen Burnie, MD 21061
301-437-2501

G. Schoepfer Inc.
460 Cook Hill Rd.
Cheshire, CT 06410
1-800-875-6939
203-250-7794 (fax)

Robert J. Smith Glass Eyes
14900 W. 31st Ave.
Golden, CO 80401
303-278-1828
303-279-2538 (fax)

Tohickon Glass Eyes
P.O. Box 15
Erwinna, PA 18920
1-800-441-5983

Molded Birds
Greenwing Enterprises
1147 Golden Olive Court
Sanibel Island, FL 33957
813-472-8666
813-472-8445 (fax)

Paints and Brushes
Beebe Hopper Arts
731 Beech Ave.
Chula Vista, CA 91910
619-420-8766

Christian J. Hummul Co.
P.O. Box 1093
Hunt Valley, MD 21030
1-800-762-0235

Winsor & Newton Ltd.
London HA3 5RH
ENGLAND

Ruby Carvers
Elkay Products Co.
1506 Sylvan Glade
Austin, TX 78745
512-441-1155

Taxidermists
Frank Newmyer
5783 Garthby
Union Lake, MI 48085
313-363-1243

Mike's Taxidermy Studio
5019 Lolly Lane
Perry Hall, MD 21128
301-256-0860

Perfection Taxidermy
5783 Garthby
Union Lake, MI 48085
313-363-1242

Wildfowl Photos
Larry Stevens Photos
3005 Pine Spring Rd.
Falls Church, VA 22042
703-560-5771

Wooden Bases
Thomas Art Bases
Ken Thomas
1909 Woodstream Dr.
York, PA 17402
717-757-2702

Complete Carving Supplies
Buck Run Carvings
Box 151, Gully Rd.
Aurora, NY 13026
315-364-8414

Northwest Carving Supply
POB 5211
216 West Ridge
Bozeman, MT 59715
406-587-8057

Woodcarvers Supply, Inc.
P.O. Box 7500
Englewood, FL 34295-7500
1-800-284-6229
813-698-0329 (fax)

Bibliography

Andrews, Laura M., and Luce, Donald T. *Francis Lee Jaques*. University of Minnesota Press. 1982.

Audubon, John James. *The Birds of America*. Crown Publishers. 1966.

Bishop, Richard, and Williams, Russ. *The Ways of Waterfowl*. J. G. Ferguson Company. 1971.

Burk, Bruce. *Complete Waterfowl Studies, Volume I—Dabbling and Whistling Ducks*. Schiffer Publishing Company. 1984.

———. *Complete Waterfowl Studies, Volume II—Diving Ducks*. Schiffer Publishing Company. 1984.

———. *Game Bird Carving*. Winchester Press. 1972.

———. *Waterfowl Studies*. Winchester Press. 1976.

Clement, Roland C. *The Living World of Audubon*. Grosset & Dunlop. 1974.

Connett, Eugene V., III. *Duck Decoys*. Durrell Publications, D. Van Nostrand. 1953.

Coykendall, Rolf. *Duck Decoys and How to Rig Them*. Holt, Rinehard and Winston. 1955.

Day, Albert M. *North American Waterfowl*. Stackpole Books. 1949.

Dermid, Jack, and Hester, Eugene. *The World of the Wood Duck*. J. B. Lippincott Company. 1973.

Dougall, Robert, and Ede, Basil. *Basil Ede's Birds*. Van Nostrand, Reinhold. 1981.

Elman, Robert. *The Atlantic Flyway*. Winchester Press. 1971.

Frank, Charles W., Jr. *Anatomy of a Waterfowl*. Pelican Publishing Company. 1982.

Gilley, Wendell H. *The Art of Bird Carving*. Hillcrest Publishers, Inc. 1972.

Hochbaum, H. Albert. *The Canvasback on a Prairie Marsh*. Stackpole Books. 1944.

———. *To Ride the Wind*. Richard Bonnycastle Book. 1973.

Hyde, Dayton O., Editor. *Raising Wild Ducks in Captivity*. E. P. Dutton and Company. 1974.

Johnsgard, Paul A. *Waterfowl*. University of Nebraska Press. 1968.

————. *Waterfowl of North America*. Indiana University Press. 1975.

Kortwright, Frank F. *Ducks, Geese and Swans of North America*. Stackpole Books. 1976.

Lansdowne, J. Fenwick. *Birds of the West Coast*. Houghton Mifflin Company. 1976.

————. *Birds of the West Coast II*. Houghton Mifflin Company, 1980.

Lansdowne, J. Fenwick, and Livingston, John A. *Birds of the Eastern Forest*. Houghton Mifflin Company. 1968.

————. *Birds of the Eastern Forest II*. Houghton Mifflin Company. 1970.

————. *Birds of the Northern Forest*. Houghton Mifflin Company, 1966.

LeMaster, Richard. *Waterfowl*. Contemporary Books, Inc. 1983.

————. *Wildlife in Wood*. Model Technology, Inc. 1978.

Line, Les. *Audubon Society Book of Wild Birds*. Harry N. Abrams. 1976.

Matthiessen, Peter. *The Shore Birds of North America*. Viking Press. 1967.

Meanley, Brooke. *Waterfowl of the Chesapeake*. Tidewater Publishing Company. 1982.

Mitchell, Alan. *Lambert's Birds of Shore and Estuary*. Scribners. 1979.

————. *Field Guide to Birds of North America*. National Geographic Society. 1983.

————. *Stalking Birds with Color Camera*. National Geographic Society. 1961.

————. *Water, Prey and Game Birds*. National Geographic Society. 1965.

Pearson, T. Gilbert, Editor-in-Chief. *Birds of America*. Garden City Books. 1917.

Peck, Robert McCracken. *A Celebration of Birds*. Walker and Company. 1982.

Peterson, Roger Tory. *A Field Guide to the Birds*. Houghton Mifflin Company, 1980.

Poole, Robert M., Editor. *The Wonder of Birds*. National Geographic Society. 1983.

Pough, Richard H. *Audubon Water Bird Guide*. Doubleday and Company. 1951.

Queeny, Edgar M. *Prairie Wings*. Ducks Unlimited. 1946.

Schroeder, Roger. *How to Carve Wildfowl*. Stackpole Books. 1984.

Scott, Peter. *Key to the Wildfowl of the World*. Wildfowl Trust. 1957.

————. *Morning Flight*. Watson and Viney Ltd. 1935.

————. *Observations of Wildlife*. Cornell University Press. 1980.

————. *Wild Chorus*. Robert Maclehose and Company Ltd. 1938.

Simon, Hilda. *The Splendor of Iridescence*. Dodd, Mead and Company. 1971.

Sowls, Lyle K. *Prairie Ducks*. Stackpole Books. 1955.

Stepanek, O. *Birds of Heath and Marshland*. West Book House. 1962.

Tawes, William I. *Creative Bird Carving*. Tidewater Publishing Company. 1969.

Terres, John K. *The Audubon Society Encyclopedia of North American Birds*. Alfred A. Knopf. 1980.

Todd, Frank S. *Waterfowl*. Harcourt Brace Jovanovich. 1979.

————. *Waterfowl Tomorrow*. U.S. Government Printing Office. 1964.

Van Wormer, Joe. *The World of the Swan*. J. B. Lippincott Company. 1972.

Veasey, Tricia. *Waterfowl Illustrated*. Schiffer Publishing Ltd. 1983.

Williamson, C. S. *Honker*. D. Van Nostrand Company, Inc. 1967.

Wright, Bruce. *High Tide and an East Wind*. Stackpole Books. 1954.